the WEEKDAY VEGETARIANS

Get Simple

FOR DAD.

the **WEEKDAY VEGETARIANS**

strategies +
so-good recipes
to suit every
craving + mood

Get Simple

Jenny Rosenstrach

New York Times bestselling author of **The Weekday Vegetarians**
and **Dinner: A Love Story**

Photographs by Christine Han

CLARKSON POTTER/PUBLISHERS
NEW YORK

Library of Congress Cataloging-in-Publication Data
is available upon request.

ISBN 978-0-593-58085-1
Ebook ISBN 978-0-593-58086-8

Printed in China

Editor: Raquel Pelzel
Editorial assistant: Elaine Hennig
Designer: Stephanie Huntwork with contributing
design work by Jan Derevjanik and lettering by
Laura Palese
Pattern illustration: Xansa/Shutterstock
Production editors: Ashley Pierce and Abby Oladipo
Production manager: Kim Tyner
Compositors: Merri Ann Morrell and Hannah Hunt
Food stylist: Lauren Radel
Prop stylist: Maeve Sheridan
Prop stylist assistant: Zach Molina
Photo assistant: Stephanie Munguia
Photo retoucher: Ché Graham
Copyeditor: Kate Slate
Proofreader: Rachel Holzman
Indexer: Thérèse Shere
Publicist: Lauren Chung
Marketer: Andrea Portanova

10 9 8 7 6 5 4 3 2 1

First Edition

Contents

Soup
&
a Side
OR

How not to
fall back
on pasta
every night

Skillet
&
Sheet Pan
Dinners
OR

Who says
Vegetarian Cooking
has to be
Complicated?

Hearty
Comfort
Food
OR

How to convince
athletes, ravenous
teenagers, and the
proverbial meat and
potatoes eater
that vegetarian food
is filling

Introduction

I had a burger last night.

The beef was Vermont-bred, grass-fed, and it was dripping with decidedly nonlocal, nonorganic American cheese and wedged inside a potato bun whose ingredient list is longer than this paragraph. We make burgers when our two daughters come home from college begging for them, or on the occasional weekend night when we feel like eating something special (in that TGIF kind of way) and don't feel like spending money on a meal we could cook better at home. My husband, Andy, has mastered the smash burger technique, using paper-thinly sliced sweet white onions to steam the meat as it sears in the pan, yielding the kind of burger that conjures up the family's first visit to In-N-Out Burger on a 2012 California trip, but also the 1970s of my youth when it was McDonald's night in my house. Have you had a smash burger lately? Wow, they taste good. And wow, are they easy. When burgers are on the menu, it's just so simple to figure out dinner: animal protein at the center of the plate + vegetable = done. No-brainer.

I'm sure you're thinking that this is a very confusing way to begin a vegetarian cookbook. Or maybe not. If you read the first volume of *The Weekday Vegetarians*, you know that plant-forward eating is the default mode when I cook during the week—but it's also punctuated by burgers and take-out shrimp tempura and pan-seared pork chops on the weekends. Because yes, we are committed to dialing back our meat consumption for all the reasons you'd expect (feeling better, saving money, combating climate change), but also: We can't quite shake our love for a roast chicken with mashed potatoes and gravy for a Sunday dinner or sitting down to Marcella Hazan's famous Bolognese on a wintry night, or salmon on the grill in July, or . . . well, you get the picture.

But I bring up that burger because I was, yet again, struck by how straightforward dinner is when meat is at the center of the plate. And I didn't really have to do anything extra to elevate it. I mean, let's face it: There's no elevating a burger, really. It's going to taste amazing no matter how you serve it.

But, with a little mindfulness, you know what else tastes amazing? The vegan miso-mushroom tacos we topped with pickled cabbage for last Monday's dinner, a flavor bomb kind of meal that would feel just as right on a Saturday night spread. So was the creamy quinoa salad, loaded with sweet snap peas and scallions and mint and asparagus, all picked up at the farmers' market in the last few weeks of May, when the good stuff finally starts to appear after a long, cold New York winter. And the crispy fried wedges we made with chickpea flour and feta and served with a sharp lemony arugula pesto. That meal lingered on my palate—in the best way—all through the next day, until dinnertime when we treated ourselves to a deep-red tomato and blue cheese tart, which, I'm not kidding, took less than 30 minutes to get on the table.

I know you're not going to believe me, but once you get in the weekday vegetarian groove, those vegetable-forward dinners (plus all the others in this book) will become as second nature to you as flipping a ground beef patty. I've written the *Dinner: A Love Story* newsletter and blog for fifteen years, and though the way I've eaten has changed a lot over that period, one thing has remained constant: My commitment to streamlining dinner and my commitment to helping readers and families see dinner as a source of pleasure instead of a source of hair-pulling and head-scratching and for-goodness-sakes-finish-your-broccoli-ing. This book continues in that tradition, highlighting all the ways vegetarian dinners can become less of a chore and more of a ritual that you can look forward to and feel good about every day. I didn't name this whole operation *Dinner: A Love Story* for nothing.

VEGETARIAN COOKING IS NOT ABOUT PUTTING IN MORE WORK. IT'S ABOUT PUTTING IN MORE THOUGHT.

This was not the way I would've described dinner in our house when we first decided to pivot to more plant-based eating six years ago. For my entire tenure as a parent and cook up to that point, the way I had always thought about dinner was the way I thought about that burger: protein (almost always from an animal) first, everything else next. Without this default strategy, I felt a little lost, compensating for the centerstage chicken, pork, or beef with two or three extra vegetarian sideshow dishes (hence, two or three times as many pots and mixing bowls to clean up afterward) or breaking out an army of small appliances on a busy weeknight to chef up a many-ingredient sauce to help that tofu along. I don't do this anymore. Once I got the basics down, I started to look at every meat-free main through my efficiency goggles and realized something important: There are ways to streamline almost every recipe, whether it means using the right store-bought ingredients to skip a time-consuming step, or using pots and prep bowls more than once to cut back on cleanup, or simply whisking up a double batch of vinaigrette or empanadas, so you save time for your future dinner-making self—economy of scale and all that. In the recipes that follow, I promise to point out all these strategies and ultimately convince you that vegetarian cooking is not about putting in more work. It's about putting in more thought.

On the other hand, maybe you are one of those cooks who thinks of dinner as a therapeutic exercise, a cook who doesn't mind extra steps or recipes that require concentrating powers that allow you to escape from things for a little while. Maybe the main obstacle preventing

you from becoming a Weekday Vegetarian is that you are feeding ravenous teenagers or ravenous athletes who will immediately open their Chipotle app if you attempt to serve them the tofu-spinach bowl you labored over. Or, maybe it's the opposite! Maybe you don't like the fact that your default mode seems to be leaning on bread and pasta and cheese (or all three!) when you decide to cook vegetarian for your family even though you crave lighter, more protein-focused meals. Maybe you've figured out how to omit meat, but what you really want to do is eat more vegetables. (Which is not always the same thing—talking to you, Pizza Night!) Maybe the issue is purely technical: Maybe you simply cannot figure out how to make meals taste flavorful without using chicken broth in the stew or bacon in the beans.

I've been writing about my transition to plant-based eating for six years, and I find that each of these obstacles can be extremely legitimate and incredibly real on any given night. So I thought long and hard about the kinds of recipes that solve specific dilemmas, which is why you'll find this book organized by the following chapters:

Soup & a Side . . .
OR HOW NOT TO FALL BACK ON PASTA EVERY NIGHT

Skillet & Sheet Pan Dinners . . .
OR WHO SAYS VEGETARIAN COOKING HAS TO BE COMPLICATED?

Hearty Comfort Food . . .
OR HOW TO CONVINCE ATHLETES, RAVENOUS TEENAGERS & THE PROVERBIAL MEAT & POTATOES EATER THAT VEGETARIAN FOOD IS FILLING

Dinner Salads & Bowls . . .
OR HOW TO EAT MORE VEGETABLES, NOT JUST EAT LESS MEAT

Pasta & Noodles . . .
OR WHEN YOU NEED TO FEED THE BEASTS

Stuffed, Wrapped & Topped . . .
OR HOW TO STOCK YOUR FREEZER, FRIDGE & PANTRY TO SPEED UP DINNER

Hooks . . .
OR MORE SAUCES, SIDES & SPARKLY THINGS THAT ADD MAJOR FLAVOR TO YOUR VEGETARIAN COOKING *

THIS BUILDS ON THE IDEA INTRODUCED IN VOLUME 1 OF THE WEEKDAY VEGETARIANS THAT THERE SHOULD ALWAYS BE ONE SLIGHTLY INDULGENT THING ON THE PLATE THAT YOU ARE TRULY EXCITED ABOUT, WHETHER IT'S A CRISPY GRILLED BREAD RUBBED WITH FRESH TOMATOES, OR CREAMY SCALLOPED POTATOES, OR THE SWEET-AND-SALTY ALMOND CLUSTERS THAT TAKE A DEPENDABLE GREEN SALAD FROM GOOD TO GREAT.

No matter what chapter you are cooking from, no matter what recipe you are making, you can assume I was looking for shortcuts and tricks to make it as easy as possible to execute. To that end, throughout these pages, look for tags that will help you with all the magic words: make-ahead, quick cleanup, freeze it, and under 30 minutes, and of course vegan.

In other words, no more excuses! Take one small step every day and before you know it, you and your family will be well on your way to becoming Weekday Vegetarians.

But First

A STARTER KIT FOR VEGETARIAN COOKING (21 INGREDIENTS, ENDLESS DINNER POSSIBILITIES)

Quesadilla with Refried Beans, Salsa, Cabbage, Cheese 20

Egg Scramble with Cheddar, Onion, Spinach 20

Crispy Chickpeas with Spinach & Yogurt 21

Pasta with Yogurt & Caramelized Onions 21

Open-Faced Grilled Cheese with Caramelized Onions and/or Pesto 22

Tostada with Egg & Pickled Onions 22

Carbonara with Cabbage & Miso 23

Pasta, Pesto, Parm 23

Mommmmmmm

. . . came the first text from Phoebe.

Any parent of a college kid is probably familiar with the mild panic attack that accompanies a text like this. If you are anything like me, during the five seconds while you stare at the three dots awaiting a follow-up, you run through all the possible scenarios of what could be wrong, while simultaneously reminding yourself that they are texting and able to put sentences together, so it can't be too terrible, right?

But I've become something of an expert on these situations and knew that the multiple Mmmmms in Mommmmm was a good sign. It suggested, perhaps, playfulness? Not like the time Phoebe's sister, Abby, who attends college in Vermont texted me:

Mom

and then . . .

I think I have a hernia

And then, ten seconds later, after I had googled "hernia general surgeon Burlington" and identified the checklist of symptoms to ask her about, she followed up with . . .

or maybe I just ate too much at lunch

But still, Phoebe's many-m'd text came the day after she arrived at the apartment in Minnesota, where she'd be living for the summer (read: 1,200 miles from her mommmm), so I stopped what I was doing to stare at the three dots, heart slowly making its way into my throat.

> **HELP!**

. . . came the next text. Why can't they just write it all in one shot? Why the drama? Then:

> **What do I cook for myself?????**

> **!!!**

Now this was my kind of text! Much better than the one I received from her a few weeks before outlining in detail a mole on her back "that has no defined edges." Or the one I screenshot and sent to my friend who is an infectious disease doctor within milliseconds of receiving it:

> **"I woke up with a weird rash, do you think it's monkey pox"**

No, this was dinner! This was my kind of problem. The best kind of problem!

Now, I'm sure you're thinking that the children of a cookbook author, kids who have grown up watching all that goes into a meal and then some, would have this piece of the adulting puzzle figured out. And they do, partly. Though neither of my daughters is particularly well versed in dermatological issues *(Mom! pretty sure I have a keloid)*, both know how to cook a very solid meal for themselves and even for a few of their lucky friends. But, as we all know, executing a meal from beginning to end, as opposed to simply cooking it, requires using an entirely different side of your brain. There is, of course, all the planning that happens before you even step into the kitchen: What staples should be in the pantry, what should be on the shopping list, what meals will fit a budget, and, of course, not *how* do I cook, but:

> **WHAT DO I COOK????**

That was a text that came a few days later from her sister, also off the college meal plan, and also cooking for herself for the first time.

I told her I was already putting together a plan for Phoebe, so I would do a little research and send it along after customizing something for Abby. If this sounds like a lot of work, let me assure you it's infinitely more fun than going down the Google rabbit hole on gastroesophageal reflux disorder. *(I have every symptom.)* The good news is that the shopping list for a college kid learning how to cook for themselves is minimal, accessible (90 percent of it can be found at any main street supermarket), easy on the wallet, and very similar to one that I'd recommend to anyone interested in experimenting with plant-forward eating. Or even to someone who is a long-time vegetarian and just wants a handful of back-pocket, low-drama, super-satisfying meals to whip up with minimal mess in not much time. Here's the short and sweet (savory?) list, and the many inspired meals you'll then be ready to cook.

THE OFFICIAL "STARTER KIT" VEGETARIAN SHOPPING LIST

Extra-virgin olive oil

Vinegar (red wine or rice)

Kosher salt and black peppercorns

Sweet white miso

Red pepper flakes

Spinach (feel free to buy this frozen so you don't have to use it immediately)

Yellow onions

Red or green cabbage (lasts forever)

Canned or dried beans: chickpeas, black beans, and white beans

Canned vegetarian refried beans (black and pinto)

Corn or flour tortillas (I recommend spending a few extra bucks on a brand of corn tortillas, like Vista Hermosa, made from masa if you can)

Good bread (slice and freeze as soon as you get home)

Pasta (your favorite shape)

Jarred marinara (we like Rao's)

Jarred salsa

Store-bought pesto (traditional or vegan)

Unsalted butter (dairy or nondairy)

Yogurt (dairy or nondairy)

A block of sharp cheddar cheese

Eggs

A hunk of real Parmigiano-Reggiano cheese (this is expensive, but a little goes a long way, and it lasts for a long time)

YOUR FIRST 8 DINNERS

① ②

Quesadilla with Refried Beans, Salsa, Cabbage, Cheese

✳ Add a **tortilla** to a little **oil** in a skillet set over medium heat, then sprinkle with enough **shredded cheese** to evenly cover and cook until the cheese starts to get melty. • Meanwhile, spread **refried beans** on another tortilla like you're spreading peanut butter on a sandwich, then invert that tortilla on top of the melted cheese tortilla. • Flip and fry the whole thing until crispy on each side. • Serve with **salsa** and **shredded cabbage** that's been tossed with **oil** and **vinegar**.

Egg Scramble with Cheddar, Onion, Spinach

✳ Whisk together 2 to 3 **eggs** with **salt** and **pepper**, **shredded cheddar**, about 2 tablespoons finely chopped **onion**, and a small handful of **spinach** (thawed and squeezed dry, if frozen). • Melt a little **butter** in a nonstick skillet over medium-low heat, add the **egg mixture**, and scramble until it reaches the desired doneness. Serve with buttered toast.

(3)

(4)

Crispy Chickpeas with Spinach & Yogurt

Pour about ¼ inch of **olive oil** into a deep skillet set over medium-high heat. • Add a can of drained **chickpeas** (dried as much as possible), **salt**, **pepper**, and **red pepper flakes** to the pan, spreading in one layer as much as possible. • Cook 6 to 8 minutes without stirring to get them nice and crispy. • Then stir in a few handfuls of **spinach** and cook another 5 minutes. • Serve in a shallow bowl on a bed of **plain yogurt** (dairy or nondairy).

Pasta with Yogurt & Caramelized Onions

In a pot of boiling **salted** water, cook a single serving of **pasta** (I prefer spaghetti or a ribbon pasta for this) according to the package directions. • Reserving ¼ cup of the pasta water, drain the pasta. • Keep the pot nearby. • Meanwhile, cook 1 sliced **onion** (seasoned with **salt** and **pepper**) in 3 tablespoons of **olive oil** in a deep skillet set over medium-low heat. • Cook until caramelized, stirring occasionally, about 15 minutes. • Add about ⅓ cup **plain yogurt** (dairy or nondairy) to the pasta pot and whisk in a little pasta water at a time until it looks saucy. • Toss in the drained **pasta** and serve with grated **Parm**, the **caramelized onions**, and **red pepper flakes**.

(5)

(6)

Open-Faced Grilled Cheese with Caramelized Onions and/or Pesto

✳ Cook 1 sliced **onion** in 2 tablespoons of **olive oil** in a deep skillet set over medium-low heat. • Season with **salt** and **pepper**. • Cook until the onion is caramelized, stirring occasionally, about 15 minutes. • Toast **bread** until it's very lightly browned, like barely showing any color. • Top with **cheddar** slices and finish on a foil-lined sheet pan under the broiler for 2 to 3 minutes, or until the cheese is melted and bubbling. • Eat topped with **onions** and/or **pesto**, if using.

Tostada with Egg & Pickled Onions

✳ Make the **pickled onions**: In a small saucepan, simmer ½ cup **water** with ½ cup **vinegar**, 2 tablespoons **sugar**, and 1 tablespoon **salt** until the sugar dissolves. • Add 1 small red or yellow **onion** (sliced) and let sit as long as possible. • Heat a few scoops of **refried beans** in a small pot. • Cook **tortillas** (preferably corn, but flour will work, too) in **oil** in a skillet set over medium heat until crispy and browned on both sides, then transfer to a paper towel. • Crack 2 **eggs** into the same pan and cook the eggs over easy or sunny-side up, whichever you like better. • Top each tostada with **beans**, **egg**, and **pickled onions**.

(7)

(8)

Carbonara with Cabbage & Miso

✳Prepare a single serving of **spaghetti** according to the package directions. • While it's boiling, whisk 1 **egg** in a medium bowl. • Reserving ¼ cup of **pasta water**, drain the spaghetti and return it to the pot while the pasta is still a little wet. • Using tongs, toss the spaghetti with 1 tablespoon of **miso** that's been thinned out with a little tap water. • Remove the pot from the heat completely. • Vigorously whisk a tablespoon or two of hot pasta water into the beaten egg to warm it—this is called "tempering." • Add the tempered egg to the pasta slowly, tossing until the pasta looks silky and coated, but not drippy and wet. • Toss in a generous sprinkle of **Parmesan** and a few handfuls of **shredded cabbage**.

Pasta, Pesto, Parm

✳Cook a single serving of **pasta** according to the package directions. • Reserving a little of the pasta water, drain the pasta and return it to the pot. • Add a few spoonfuls of **pesto** and some grated **Parm**, then toss, using the reserved pasta water to help distribute the sauce. • Serve topped with more **cheese** and a generous drizzle of **olive oil**.

AND YOUR NEXT 20 DINNER POSSIBILITIES . . .

that are so simple, you can figure out how to make them using just their names and all can be made from the starter kit shopping list on page 19. Many become vegan-friendly if you drop the cheddar or Parm.

Simmered Brothy Lima Beans
with Miso

Breakfast Quesadillas
with Eggs, Cheddar & Salsa

Spinach & Onion Omelet

Cheese & Salsa Quesadilla

Scrambled Eggs on Toast with
Caramelized Onions

Open-Faced Cheddar Toast with
Spinach & Caramelized Onions

Open-Faced Cheddar Toast with
Miso-Caramelized Onions

White Beans with Vegan Pesto
(vegan)

Seven-Minute Eggs
with Pesto & Toast

Toaster Oven Pizza with
Good Bread, Parm & Marinara

Shakshuka
(Eggs Baked in Marinara)

Pasta with Marinara & Parm

Pasta with Chickpeas,
Olive Oil, Pepper, Parm

Grilled Cheddar with Pesto

Pasta con Ceci
(Pasta with Marinara & Chickpeas)
(vegan)

Cacio e Pepe
(Pasta with Cheese and Pepper)

Caramelized Cabbage
with Fried Egg & Toast

Miso-Roasted Cabbage with
Chickpeas (vegan)

Migas (Pan-Fried Tortillas,
Eggs, Cheese & Salsa)

Whisked Egg & Onion Miso Soup

1 Trader Joe's 10 Minute Farro

For me, it's worth the extra trip to Trader Joe's just to stock up on bags of this quick-cook whole grain. The stuff is lifesaving. You cook it like pasta, bringing a pot of water to a boil and simmering for 10 minutes—just enough time to prepare whatever vegetables you plan to toss with it. (You could also use this in place of the farro piccolo in Farro Piccolo with Crispy Mushrooms & Parm, page 134.) It aids and abets Crunchy Stuffed Red Peppers (page 196); we also frequently serve it with Parm, a drizzle of olive oil, and some form of egg (fried, 7-minute, etc.) for a nutritious, delicious, 15-minute vegetarian dinner.

2 Pizza Dough

I know! It's so easy to make your own pizza dough, but pizza dough calls for advance planning as well as yeast, which, I'm sorry, is inherently a scary word. Also? Hot take: The store-bought kind you find in the refrigerated sections of most supermarkets is low-key usually *better than homemade*. I always have an army of 16-ouncers in my freezer. It is so satisfying to take one out in the morning or early afternoon, cover it with a dry kitchen towel, and know it will be thawed and ready to go for say, that Sheet Pan Pizza with Asparagus, Boursin & Spring Onions on page 189.

3 Precooked Rice (White and Brown)

Even after decades of cooking, it still feels like a small miracle when rice from scratch comes out perfect enough to fluff with a fork. The frozen precooked kind eliminates any stress around that, but more important, it gives me the option to always have vegetable fried rice in the dinner rotation, instead of only those days when I have leftover rice (day-old rice = optimal fried rice).

4 Precooked Beets

We used to buy shrink-wrapped, precooked, previnegared beets mostly because the girls would pop them in their mouths like candy for an after-school snack. But soon enough I got so used to having them around that I started tossing them into green salads, grain salads, and whirling them into bright beautiful pink hummus. The thing is: I know exactly how to roast fresh beets so they come out just right every time (roast them wrapped in foil at 375°F for 1 hour 15 minutes, let cool, slip off skins with fingers), but . . . it requires 1 hour 15 minutes and some concentrated hand-washing.

5 Refrigerated Pie Crust and Puff Pastry

If it's Thanksgiving or a special occasion, I'm going full-out, never-fail, Martha Stewart *pâte brisée* (aka tart dough), but for a regular old Tuesday night? I put my money on store-bought every time. (Pillsbury is my favorite.) I use them for savory galettes (like that butternut squash number on page 119) and pot pies. For puff pastry, I seek out the Dufour brand, which is all-butter (not shortening). If you have that in the fridge you are halfway done with making the Golden Greens Pie (page 113) and the Roasted Tomato Tart (page 109), and you are always just a thaw away from any kind of roast vegetable tart.

6 Empanada Discs

Once you have the basics for baked empanadas down (and the Baked Pinto Bean Empanadas on page 186 are an excellent place to start), and once you start reliably replenishing your supply of frozen empanada discs, the possibilities will seem endless. They are also incredibly convenient if you're feeding a vegetarian hold-out at the table— it's easy to stuff one with chicken or sausage, while you stick to beans for the others.

7 Rao's Jarred Marinara Sauce

Rao's is the only jarred sauce I'd ever consider buying. With its bright orange hue and fresh tomatoey-basil flavor, it was the decisive victor in a jarred pasta sauce taste test I conducted a few years ago for the lifestyle website *Cup of Jo*.

8 Baked Tofu

Unlike regular extra-firm tofu, baked (sometimes seasoned) tofu already has all its moisture expelled, and it crisps up in an oiled skillet quickly. Because it is so quick-cooking, I often fry up a few slices for lunch, surrounding it with sautéed vegetables. No stopping you from doing the same at dinner. I'm not particularly loyal to any one brand, but Wildwood and Nasoya are the ones I pick up the most often.

9 Gotham Greens Pesto

I've never found a jarred pesto that didn't require a squeeze of fresh lemon juice to raise its quality to just barely mediocre. And making pesto yourself can sometimes be both a pain and expensive. (Why are pine nuts so pricey?) But when it's good—and Gotham Greens is good—it's like owning a new pair of black pants that you want to wear with everything. The pesto is good on pasta, obviously, but also mixed into soups, spread on sandwiches, heaped onto braised beans, and baked into simple pesto pizzas. You should also feel free to drizzle this over the Spicy Feta Chickpea Wedges (page 84) in place of the arugula pesto.

10 Marinated Artichokes (and Marinated Beans)

Whether you buy them in the simple glass jar that you find on a shelf in the canned vegetable aisle of your supermarket or at the Italian salumeria or pack them yourself from your grocery store's salad bar, either way, this is a two-for-one ingredient. You can use the marinade as the starting point (and sometimes even the ending point!) for dressing, which is helpful if you're cooking in a vacation rental and you don't feel like buying a bunch of ingredients that you won't need for very long. Marinated beans are also excellent to turn to in that situation.

11 Precubed Butternut Squash

It's true that almost every vegetable that comes presliced is bagged or contained in plastic, which is an environmental nightmare, so I do my best to limit myself to the ones I feel most strongly about, and butternut squash is one of them. Saving time on the peeling, seeding, and chopping is appreciated, of course, but I also do find that it's one of the more reliably flavorful precubed vegetables. Especially if you buy organic. (And if you dislike the dry fuzziness that results from handling squash and pumpkins, you get to avoid that, too.)

12 Garlic Salt or Powder

When I was first figuring out my way around a kitchen, I remember reading that "real cooks" never use prepeeled garlic. The basic argument: You never know how fresh it is; peeled cloves go rancid more quickly than unpeeled; unless you work in an Italian restaurant you'll end up wasting half of them etc., etc. I don't even remember where I read that advice, but to this day, I find myself glaring at the shoppers buying prepeeled garlic as though they're puppy haters. And then, all pleased with myself, I head to the spice section in the next aisle and drop a jar of garlic salt in my shopping cart. I'm guessing that if my grandmothers Catrino and Turano were still alive, the first thing they'd do is toss my book in the trash after reading this. It's not that I don't use fresh garlic, I just use garlic salt for a few select tasks that I'm seemingly performing all the time: Brushing the perimeter of a pizza dough with a mixture of olive oil and garlic salt, sprinkling it on a buttered baguette with Parm and baking it into garlic bread, whirling it into a dressing on those nights I just can't deal with breaking out the garlic press—otherwise known as 100 percent of nights.

TRADER JOE'S®
10 Minute
FARRO
10
PRE-COOKED & QUICK COOK

NET WT. 8.8 OZ
(249g)

V

SERVING
SUGGESTION

Make It
Savory

Pillsbury

Pie
Crusts

Make It
Sweet

2 Crusts
Like Homemade Without the Hassle

NET WT
14.1 OZ (399g)

PER 1/8
CRUST:

100
CALORIES

2.5g
SAT FAT

130mg

0g
TOTAL
SUGARS

red®
ed

USDA
ORGANIC

Delicate, Nutty
and Zesty

BEST IF
USED

Peel & Reseal

Love™
BEETS

Perfectly Pickled

BEETS

SLICED & Ready
to Eat!

SLIGHTLY
SWEET
and great in
salads, sandwiches,
snacks & more!

Best Before
28 Sep 23
NET WT.
8 oz (226g)

KEEP REFRIGERATED

PIZZA

PIZZA DOUGH

NET WT 15 OZ (1 lb) 454g

QUICKEST ANTIPASTO
BAR SALAD (PAGE 59)

SOUP & SALAD, SPRING EDITION:
STREAMLINED MUSHROOM SOUP + QUICKEST
ANTIPASTO BAR SALAD

STREAMLINED
MUSHROOM SOUP
(PAGE 39)

Soup

&

a Side

OR

How not to
fall back
on pasta
every night

Recipes

OF ALL THE REASONS NOT TO GO VEGETARIAN, the Carb-Crutch Issue is probably the one I hear about the most. *When there's no meat on the plate, I end up relying on pasta most nights or bread to fill up,* people say. Or: *The only vegetarian meals my kids would ever eat are pasta and pizza, and I don't want to eat like that every night.* Well I don't either. But not because I have anything against carbs—in my house, we are adoring fans of our cacio e pepes and Margherita pizzas. But, because we are human, i.e., not the same kind of eater with the same kind of cravings every single night of our lives, we also appreciate a meal that relies as much on plant-forward flavor and freshness as it does on crusty baguettes and baked pastas.

Enter: The Soup and Side Dinner, which, yes, does require you to make two separate recipes, but in almost all cases, the salad or the side comes together while the soup is simmering (or, occasionally, the opposite), meaning you still end up minimizing time spent stressing over the stovetop. Best of all, this way of thinking about dinner really helps you take advantage of in-season produce—here's a case where the recipes really let the vegetables be the star.

THE IMPORTANCE OF A BLENDER AND BROTH

There are two things I feel the need to endorse before you head into this chapter. First: A solid blender. Yes, it is always easier to plunge an immersion blender into a pot of softened, brothy vegetables when you're after a certain creamy soup consistency (and you should absolutely do this if breaking out the big blender is going to stop your dinner momentum altogether), but pureeing those vegetables in a powerful blender will almost always result in a silkier, richer consistency and overall, a good quality blender, like a Cuisinart or Vitamix, is going to be an investment that greatly pays off.

Second: I call for vegetable broth in many of these soup recipes. If you read my first *Weekday Vegetarians* cookbook, you know I prefer even the most bare-bones homemade vegetable broth over any carton of store-bought broth, which, to me, always carries the slight whiff of . . . shall we say . . . marsh? But, of course, if the name of the game here is weeknight fast, it's not exactly fair of me to assume people have time to simmer a bunch of carrots, onions, and celery on the stovetop all afternoon (or even for 30 minutes). Enter: Better Than Bouillon, the roasted vegetable base that comes in little jars in your supermarket soup section. I resisted trying it for so long because it is pretty high in sodium, but once I got used to its savory depth, I had a hard time going back. Even to my homemade version! So when I call for vegetable broth in these recipes, of course homemade is best, but in a pinch, Better Than Bouillon is what I recommend.

MIX + MATCH

SIDES → / SOUPS →	Homiest Roasted Tomato Soup	Smoky Tomato-White Bean Soup	Streamlined Mushroom Soup	Shortcut Minestrone
Kale & Roasted Delicata Squash Salad with Sweet and Spicy Tahini Dressing	★	★	★	
Diced Cucumber Salad with Tomatoes, Watermelon & Feta				
Sliced Orange Salad with Fennel & Shallots		★	★	★
Crispy Sweet Potatoes with Lemon-Yogurt Dressing & Dukkah	★		★	
Crispy Curried Cauliflower with Coconut & Raisins	★		★	
Gem Lettuce Salad with Honey-Sea Salt Almonds & Gorgonzola		★		
Butter-Fried Cabbage with Apples	★		★	
Avocado-Cucumber Salad with Carrot-Ginger Dressing & Chives	★			
Blasted Artichokes with Yogurt-Dill Dressing			★	
One-Pan Spaghetti Squash with Tomatoes & Burrata			★	
Quickest Antipasto-Bar Salad	★	★	*SPRING PICK (SEE PHOTO PAGE 30)*	
Pomegranate-Glazed Eggplant with Whipped Feta		★		
Sliced Avocado Salad with Arugula & Crispy Capers	★	★		★
Sugar Snap Pea Salad Two Ways			★	
Choose-Your-Own-Adventure Slaw		★		
Roasted Vegetables with Miso Butter			★	★

SOUP + SIDE

Pureed Broccoli Soup with Romesco & Frizzled Onions	Coconut-Corn Soup with Tofu, Basil & Chiles	Vegetarian Avgolemeno	Strawberry-Tomato Gazpacho with Feta
		★	
	★	★	
★		★	
FALL PICK (SEE PHOTO PAGE 45)		★	
★		★	★
	★	★	
★			
	★		
★		★	
		★	★
	★		
★	★		*SUMMER PICK (SEE PHOTO PAGE 51)*
	★		
	WINTER PICK (SEE PHOTO PAGE 48)		

HOW IT WORKS

1. Pick a Soup
Craving something cozy or something refreshing? Also, consider what's in season as you choose.

2. Pick a Side
Head down the soup's column to see which sides I recommend going along with that soup.

3. Start Cooking
Most of the time, the soup can be prepared while the side is in the oven, or the side can be prepared while the soup is simmering. Figure out which way is the most efficient for your chosen combo and start cooking.

Homiest
Roasted Tomato Soup

QUICK CLEANUP | FREEZE IT | VEGAN

SERVES 2
(LARGE BOWLS)
OR 4
(SMALL BOWLS)

I love this soup for its flavor, but I might love it more for its ease—you just throw the seasoned tomatoes, shallots, garlic, and rosemary onto a parchment- or foil-lined sheet pan, then slide the finished, roasted, concentrated contents of that sheet pan into a blender, skins and all. I make this all year long, even in the winter, when tomatoes are decidedly off-season—they sweeten up when roasted—because what is more cozy and comforting on a cold night than tomato soup? In the summer, when tomatoes are extra sweet, I often stir in a tablespoon of sherry vinegar for a little brightness. (Off-season tomatoes are usually acidic enough without it.) It's wonderful when rounded out with salad (see chart, pages 34–35), a shower of freshly grated Parm, or an optional grilled cheese—the Juliet to tomato soup's Romeo.

10 plum tomatoes, quartered

2 medium shallots, peeled but whole (or 4 shallot halves that are roughly the same size as the quartered tomatoes)

2 garlic cloves, peeled but whole

2 fresh rosemary sprigs

Kosher salt and freshly ground black pepper to taste

¼ cup plus 3 tablespoons extra-virgin olive oil

¼ teaspoon Calabrian chili powder

⅓ cup vegetable broth, plus more as needed

Sherry vinegar (optional)

1 Preheat the oven to 400°F. Line a sheet pan with foil or parchment paper.

2 Place the tomatoes, shallots, garlic cloves, and rosemary on the lined pan. Season with salt and pepper and drizzle with 3 tablespoons of the olive oil, tossing with your hands to make sure everything is slick and shiny.

3 Roast until the tomato skins shrivel a little and darken and the shallots turn slightly golden, 30 to 35 minutes. Remove from the oven and let sit for a few minutes to cool, then discard the rosemary sprigs.

4 Using your hands, pick up the foil or parchment at the corners and slide the roasted tomatoes (and the aromatics and juices) into the blender. Add the remaining ¼ cup olive oil, chili powder, and the broth and puree until smooth and vibrant. You might want to add a few more tablespoons of broth (or water) if the puree is too thick. Taste and adjust for seasoning with sherry vinegar (if using) or more salt and pepper if needed.

Smoky Tomato-White Bean Soup

FREEZE IT

SERVES 4

I've made a version of tomato and white bean soup for so many years that it's become one of those recipes I don't even really think of as cookbook-worthy or even newsworthy. That is, until one afternoon last year, when my brother and sister-in-law came over for a weekend winter lunch. At the last minute, I pulled this soup together (that's what it's great for; it's the *epitome* of a pantry-raid meal), adding a little smoky paprika just for fun, and reserving a few beans at the end for more texture. These simple additions unlocked something and I suddenly found myself making the soup not just for weekend on-the-fly lunches, but also for nights when dinner was a scramble, or when friends were going through a rough patch and needed some comfort in the form of soup.

3 tablespoons extra-virgin olive oil

1 small yellow onion, finely chopped

2 medium carrots, finely chopped

1 celery stalk, finely chopped

2 garlic cloves, minced

1 tablespoon smoked paprika

Kosher salt and freshly ground black pepper to taste

2 (15-ounce) cans white beans, such as cannellini or Great Northern, drained, **or 1½ cups cooked white beans**

1 (14.5-ounce) can diced tomatoes, undrained

2 cups vegetable broth, homemade or Better Than Bouillon

Freshly grated Parmesan cheese

1 In a medium soup pot, heat the oil over medium heat. Stir in the onion, carrots, celery, garlic, paprika, salt, and pepper and cook, stirring occasionally, until the vegetables are soft, 5 to 8 minutes.

2 Set ½ cup of beans aside and add the rest to the pot. Add the diced tomatoes with their juices and the vegetable broth. Increase the heat slightly until the liquid comes to a simmer, and cook until everything is warmed through, about 3 minutes. Remove from the heat.

3 Using an immersion blender, blend the soup until it's smooth, adding water if necessary if it's too thick for your taste (blend in batches if needed). Set the pot over low heat and simmer about 15 minutes to allow the flavors to deepen. During the last few minutes, stir in the reserved beans and cook until warmed through.

4 Serve topped with Parmesan.

TO VEGANIZE: OMIT THE PARM

Streamlined Mushroom Soup

FREEZE IT

SERVES 4

My friend Jenn turned me onto *Moosewood*'s Hungarian Mushroom Soup a ways back, and I immediately fell for it. The soup is hearty and flavorful enough to work as the entirety of dinner, so long as there is some crusty bread keeping it company. The only thing? It required a separate pot for the béchamel, and béchamel is what I would call a weeknight deal-breaker, so I experimented with ways to avoid that step. Turns out, it reaches the same rich consistency if you just whisk in a slurry of flour and milk. Other tweaks: mushroom powder and white wine for the simmering broth, which gets you to the desired flavor depth faster. As for mushrooms, most of the time I use supermarket creminis, but it goes without saying that market-fresh maitake, shiitake, or wild morels will take it to the next level.

3 tablespoons unsalted butter

1 pound mushrooms, any kind, thinly sliced

1 medium yellow onion, chopped

Kosher salt and freshly ground black pepper to taste

2 tablespoons mushroom powder

½ cup dry white wine or vegetable broth

1 tablespoon soy sauce

1 tablespoon sweet paprika

2 tablespoons all-purpose flour

1 cup whole milk

3 cups vegetable broth, homemade or Better Than Bouillon

1 tablespoon sherry vinegar

½ cup plain Greek yogurt (preferably 2% fat or higher)

¼ cup fresh dill or parsley, chopped

1 In a large soup pot, melt the butter over medium heat. Add half of the mushrooms and cook until shrunken a bit, about 5 minutes. Add the rest and cook until all the mushrooms lose most of their moisture, another 5 minutes. Make a clearing in the middle of the pot and add the onion and salt and pepper. Cook until onions are soft, about 5 minutes. Stir in the mushrooms from the perimeter, and add the mushroom powder, wine, soy sauce, and paprika. Cook until the mushrooms absorb most of the liquid, about 1 minute.

2 Add the flour to a small bowl and slowly whisk in the milk to make a lump-free slurry. Add the slurry to the soup pot and increase the heat to medium-high, letting it boil gently and thicken for 1 to 2 minutes. Reduce to a simmer as soon as it looks slightly thickened. Add the vegetable broth, bring to a boil, then simmer, stirring occasionally, for another 15 minutes.

3 Stir in the vinegar and serve with salt and pepper, a dollop of yogurt, and fresh herbs.

PHOTOGRAPH ON PAGE 30

Shortcut Minestrone

QUICK CLEANUP

SERVES 4

Decades ago, my friend Pilar, an amazing cook, pointed me in the direction of an authentic minestrone recipe from Giuliano Bugialli's famous cookbook *The Fine Art of Italian Cooking,* and I have to say, one of the great pleasures of life is reserving a nice stretch of hours on a Sunday to soak beans, prep a *ton* of vegetables, and then enjoy the hearty stew a few hours later for the most comforting family dinner. But what happens when the minestrone craving calls on, say, a weeknight? In this cheater's version, I use canned beans and one of those 12-ounce bags of preshredded vegetables you see at the supermarket—the ones usually deployed for slaws—to save precious weeknight minutes. Wholesome and comforting, this minestrone is filling enough and vegetable-packed enough to be the only thing on the table. And if there are any leftovers, fold them into pasta the next day for classic ribollita. Bugialli would totally approve.

2 tablespoons unsalted butter

1 tablespoon extra-virgin olive oil, plus more for drizzling

1 large yellow onion, thinly sliced

Kosher salt and freshly ground black pepper to taste

1 garlic clove, minced

¼ teaspoon red pepper flakes

1 tablespoon tomato paste

2 (15-ounce) cans white beans, such as cannellini, drained and rinsed

4 cups vegetable broth, homemade or Better Than Bouillon

1 (14.5-ounce) can diced tomatoes, undrained

1 (12-ounce) bag shredded slaw vegetables (or 5 cups of your own shredded vegetables such as cabbage, broccoli, carrots, cauliflower, etc.)

1 tablespoon sherry vinegar, plus more to taste

Handful of fresh basil leaves, torn, for serving

Freshly grated or shaved Parmesan cheese, for serving

1 In a medium pot, melt the butter with the olive oil over medium-high heat. Add the onion and season with salt and pepper. Cook until they're nicely browned and frizzled (don't stir too much), 8 to 10 minutes. Using a slotted spoon, transfer one-quarter of the onions to a small bowl and set aside (you'll use this as a topping). Add the garlic and red pepper flakes to the remaining onion in the pot and cook until golden and aromatic, about another minute. Add the tomato paste and cook another minute, until it deepens in color and looks toasty.

2 Reduce the heat to medium, add the beans, and season with salt and pepper. Using a fork or potato masher, smash roughly half of the beans in the pot, breaking them up to release their starch (this is what will thicken the soup). Add the broth and tomatoes and bring to a boil. Reduce to a simmer and cook until the texture has thickened, about 15 minutes.

3 Stir in the shredded vegetables and the vinegar. Simmer until the vegetables have wilted, 10 to 15 minutes. Taste and season with salt, pepper, and more vinegar if you like.

4 Remove from the heat and stir in the basil. Serve in bowls topped with the reserved frizzled onions, a hefty drizzle of olive oil, some Parm, and freshly ground black pepper.

TO VEGANIZE: REPLACE THE BUTTER WITH EXTRA-VIRGIN OLIVE OIL AND OMIT THE PARM FOR SERVING

SHORTCUT MINESTRONE

Pureed Broccoli Soup
WITH Romesco & Frizzled Onions

QUICK CLEANUP | UNDER 30 MINUTES

SERVES 2
(LARGE BOWLS)
OR 4
(SMALL BOWLS)

I know I'm risking the very real problem of paralysis of choice here, but you can use this template for so many vegetables—swap out the broccoli for butternut squash, cauliflower, carrots, asparagus, even cabbage (red *or* green). Adding the extra olive oil at the end makes the soup more velvety and indulgent (obviously), and you can also experiment with drizzling in coconut milk at the end for a slightly sweeter, more filling meal. The recipe scales up easily—just make sure to use a larger pot if you do so.

¼ cup plus
2 tablespoons
extra-virgin
olive oil

1 small yellow
onion, chopped

1 garlic clove,
minced

Dash of red
pepper flakes

Kosher salt and
freshly ground
black pepper
to taste

1 pound broccoli,
florets and stems
(shave any rough
patches off the
stems with a knife
or a vegetable
peeler), roughly
chopped

4 cups vegetable
broth, homemade
or Better Than
Bouillon, plus up to
½ cup for blending

Frizzled Onions
(page 224)

Romesco Sauce
(page 228)

1 In a soup pot, heat 2 tablespoons of the olive oil over medium heat. Add the onion, garlic, pepper flakes, salt, and black pepper. Cook, stirring occasionally, until the onions are soft, about 3 minutes. Add the broccoli and broth. Increase the heat and bring to a boil, then reduce to a simmer and cook until the broccoli is very soft, 6 to 8 minutes.

2 Remove from the heat. Using a slotted spoon, remove about 1 cup of broccoli florets and set aside. Add the remaining ¼ cup olive oil to the pot with the soup. Remove the soup from the heat and let it cool slightly. Using an immersion blender or a regular blender (in batches), puree until silky and smooth, adding more broth (or water) if you prefer a brothier consistency. (If using a regular blender, make sure the steam vent on the lid is slightly ajar, to allow for some steam to escape and to prevent a pressure buildup.) Return the soup to the pot to warm through if necessary. Roughly chop the reserved broccoli.

3 Serve garnished with the reserved broccoli, frizzled onions, and romesco.

✳ *TO VEGANIZE: OPT FOR THE OLIVE OIL WHEN MAKING THE FRIZZLED ONIONS*

PUREED BROCCOLI SOUP

CRISPY CURRIED CAULIFLOWER
WITH COCONUT & RAISINS

SOUP & SALAD, FALL EDITION:
PUREED BROCCOLI SOUP + CRISPY CURRIED
CAULIFLOWER WITH COCONUT & RAISINS

Coconut-Corn Soup
with Tofu, Basil & Chiles

MAKE-AHEAD | VEGAN

SERVES 4

If there was a dessert chapter in the book you are holding, I'd consider moving this vegan soup there. The only thing preventing that is the way the chiles and lime manage to mellow the sweetness of the corn and coconut. It's just as delicious chilled as it is warm, something to consider on one of those dog days of August, when the corn is at its sweetest, and the stove is best turned on as early in the day as possible.

1 (14- or 16-ounce) package extra-firm tofu, drained, cut into ½-inch cubes

Kosher salt to taste

2 tablespoons neutral oil, such as grapeseed or canola

1 small yellow onion, chopped

Dash of red pepper flakes

Freshly ground black pepper to taste

1 large garlic clove, minced

2 teaspoons turmeric

4½ cups fresh corn kernels (from about 8 ears)

6 cups vegetable broth (or water, or some combination of the two)

⅔ cup full-fat coconut milk

2 tablespoons soy sauce

Handful of fresh basil leaves, torn

1 small Thai red chile pepper or jalapeño (including seeds and pith as desired for heat), thinly sliced into rounds

Lime wedges, for squeezing

1 Season the tofu with salt and transfer to a kitchen or paper towel to drain for 10 to 15 minutes.

2 In a medium soup pot, set over medium heat, add the oil, onion, pepper flakes, salt, and black pepper. Cook until the onions are soft, about 4 minutes. Add the garlic and turmeric and cook for another 2 minutes, until the turmeric gets toasty. Stir in 4 cups of the corn kernels and the broth, bring to an aggressive simmer, and cook until everything has softened, 8 to 10 minutes. Remove from the heat and stir in the coconut milk and soy sauce.

3 Working in batches, puree the soup in a blender until smooth (see Note). Return the soup to the pot, stir in the reserved tofu, and cook on low heat until the tofu has warmed through and absorbed some of the flavor from the broth, about 6 minutes. Ladle into soup bowls. Top with the basil, reserved corn, and chiles and serve with a lime wedge for squeezing.

NOTE: Even the most powerful blender will leave you with some fibrous corn texture here, which I don't mind. If you do, you can pass it through a fine-mesh sieve before adding the tofu.

Miso-Avocado
& Cucumber Soup

MAKE-AHEAD | QUICK CLEANUP | UNDER 30 MINUTES

SERVES 2
(LARGE BOWLS)
OR 4
(SMALL BOWLS)

This soup is as easy to make as a breakfast smoothie. It's ideal in the summer, on a night when you can't bear to turn on the oven, and also equally satisfying in the winter, when you're looking for a green, bright, flavorful reset from buttery stews, pasta bakes, or weekend meat-eating (ahem). I used to make this with chicken broth and regular garden cucumbers, which required peeling and seeding. Now I just use water (the miso lends it enough depth) and English seedless cucumbers because I can just chuck 'em into the blender without any prep.

2 avocados, halved and pitted

2 large English (seedless) cucumbers, 1 roughly chopped and 1 finely minced

1 cup plain whole-milk yogurt

2 tablespoons white miso

Juice of 1 large lime

1 small jalapeño, minced (pith and seeds removed for less heat)

5 scallions, white and light-green parts only, roughly chopped

⅓ cup roughly chopped fresh cilantro, plus more for garnish

Kosher salt and freshly ground black pepper to taste

Frizzled Onions (page 224)

Scoop the avocado into a blender. Add the roughly chopped cucumber (not the finely minced), the yogurt, miso, lime juice, jalapeño, scallions, cilantro, salt, pepper, and 1 cup water. Puree until smooth, adding more water if necessary until the mixture reaches a gazpacho-like consistency. This is extra great chilled for at least 1 hour, but it's fine at room temperature, too. (You might have to thin it out with a little more water after chilling.) Serve with the minced cucumber on top along with the frizzled onions, cilantro, and more salt and pepper to taste. Refrigerate leftovers.

TO VEGANIZE: REPLACE THE WHOLE-MILK YOGURT WITH PLAIN NONDAIRY YOGURT AND USE THE OLIVE OIL OPTION WHEN MAKING THE FRIZZLED ONIONS

ROASTED VEGETABLES
WITH MISO BUTTER

SOUP & SALAD, WINTER EDITION:
VEGETARIAN AVGOLEMONO + ROASTED VEGETABLES
WITH MISO BUTTER

VEGETARIAN AVGOLEMONO

Vegetarian Avgolemono

QUICK CLEANUP | UNDER 30 MINUTES

SERVES 2 (LARGE BOWLS) OR 4 (SMALL BOWLS)

As with traditional avgolemono (Greek chicken soup with egg and lemon), this vegetarian version also relies on eggs to give it that wonderful richness. (P.S. Did the protein police catch that one: Eggs!) And thanks to all the usual flavor-bomb things going on—dill, lemon—it's one of those go-to meals that ends up being way more than the sum of its parts. Best of all, it only takes 15 minutes.

4 cups vegetable broth, homemade or Better Than Bouillon

¼ cup orzo pasta

Kosher salt and freshly ground black pepper to taste

3 large eggs

3 tablespoons fresh lemon juice

¼ cup finely chopped fresh dill, or more to taste

1 In a large saucepan, bring the broth to a boil. Add the orzo and cook according to the package directions until tender but still al dente (the kind I use takes about 7 minutes). Season with salt and pepper and reduce the heat to a simmer.

2 While the orzo simmers, in a medium bowl, whisk together the eggs and lemon juice until smooth. While constantly whisking, slowly drizzle about 1 cup of the hot broth into the egg/lemon mixture.

3 Slowly pour the warmed egg/lemon/ broth mixture into the simmering broth and orzo in the saucepan, stirring just until the soup becomes opaque and thickens as the eggs cook, 1 to 2 minutes. Taste and season with salt if needed. Remove from the heat and serve topped with dill and a grind of pepper.

Strawberry-Tomato Gazpacho
WITH Feta

QUICK CLEANUP | UNDER 30 MINUTES

SERVES 2
(LARGE BOWLS)
OR 4
(SMALL BOWLS
OR CUPS)

In a perfect world, every late-summer tomato would be juicy and sweet, flavorful enough to eat as simply as possible—on a piece of toast with mayo or alongside mozzarella—lest you distract from the peak freshness experience. It's only fair, right? We go eleven months out of the year tolerating the subpar grape tomatoes and Styrofoam-like midwinter Romas. But alas, even in late August, when you think you've scored some good ones—you can end up with a bushel of mediocrity. That's where I found myself one 90-degree-plus-humidity day, having scored a few at the farmers' market and craving a smooth, Seville-style gazpacho that the *New York Times* first brought to my attention. But this time, faced with a bunch of good-not-great beefsteaks and cherries, I decided to deploy a trick I once saw on a fancy hotel menu: I whirled some strawberries into the blender with the rest of the produce. Not too many of them (my husband: "I don't want dessert"), but just enough to steer the blend toward a tart-sweetness. I topped the bowls with minced cucumber and strawberries and now it's my preferred gazpacho, no matter what kind of tomatoes I'm working with.

2 pounds tomatoes, any kind (I use beefsteak, heirloom, cherry, Roma, all of them), roughly chopped

1½ cups strawberries, hulled and roughly chopped

2 medium cucumbers, halved, peeled, and seeded, 1 roughly chopped and 1 diced

1 small green bell pepper or cubanelle pepper, cut into chunks

1 small yellow onion or shallot, cut into chunks

½ cup extra-virgin olive oil

1 tablespoon sherry vinegar, plus more to taste

Kosher salt to taste

4 to 5 shakes of hot sauce, or to taste

1 to 2 ounces feta cheese (optional), crumbled or cut into small cubes

Freshly ground black pepper, for serving

1   In a blender, combine the tomatoes, 1 cup of the strawberries, the roughly chopped cucumber, the bell pepper, and onion and process on high speed until emulsified and creamy, about 1 minute. Add the olive oil, vinegar, and salt and process for another 30 seconds.

2   Taste to make sure it's the right balance of sweet and acidic. (This will vary depending on the flavor of your tomatoes.) Stir in more vinegar if you think it needs a little brightness, then stir in the hot sauce.

3   Divide into bowls and serve sprinkled with feta (if using), the diced cucumber, the remaining chopped strawberries, and a few grinds of black pepper.

TO VEGANIZE: OMIT THE FETA

STRAWBERRY-TOMATO
GAZPACHO WITH FETA

SOUP & SALAD, SUMMER EDITION:
STRAWBERRY-TOMATO GAZPACHO WITH FETA &
SPICY PEANUT SUGAR SNAP PEA SALAD

SPICY PEANUT SUGAR SNAP PEA
SALAD

Kale & Roasted Delicata Squash Salad
with Sweet and Spicy Tahini Dressing

MAKE-AHEAD

SERVES 2 (LARGE BOWLS) OR 4 (SMALL BOWLS)

The crisp-fresh element of kale, red onions, and mint here plays nicely with the sweet-rich MVP of fall: delicata squash, which can be replaced with butternut if you want, but why, when you don't even have to peel the delicata?! The roasting part takes a bit of time, but the squash is just as good, if not better, at room temperature, so feel free to meal-prep it in advance. P.S. I've had great success stretching out the leftovers (kale and all) with quinoa.

1 small delicata squash, halved lengthwise, seeded, and sliced crosswise into ½-inch-thick half-moons

¼ cup extra-virgin olive oil

Kosher salt and freshly ground black pepper to taste

1 bunch Tuscan (lacinato) kale, stems and midribs removed, leaves stacked, rolled, and thinly sliced into confetti-like strands

3 tablespoons minced red onion (about ½ small red onion)

3 tablespoons salted roasted sunflower seeds

¼ cup chopped fresh mint

½ cup Sweet and Spicy Tahini Dressing (page 206)

1   Preheat the oven to 400°F. Line a sheet pan with parchment paper.

2   Add the squash, olive oil, and some salt and pepper to the sheet pan and use your hands to mix until all the squash pieces are lightly coated. Roast until the squash is tender and looks golden and shiny, about 35 minutes, flipping halfway through. Remove the sheet pan from the oven to cool.

3   In a large bowl, combine the kale, onion, sunflower seeds, mint, and cooled squash. Season with salt and pepper and toss. Drizzle with the tahini dressing and serve.

TO VEGANIZE: USE MAPLE SYRUP IN PLACE OF HONEY IN THE DRESSING

Diced Cucumber Salad *WITH* Tomatoes, Watermelon & Feta

UNDER 30 MINUTES

SERVES 2
(LARGE BOWLS)
OR 4
(SMALL BOWLS)

Even though salads are technically a one-bowl, often no-cook dish, a well-considered salad isn't always an easy-breezy proposition. You have to wash and dry the lettuce, you usually have to make a dressing; and if it's a dinner salad, there can be a cooking component like hard-boiling eggs or roasting tofu or vegetables. I think that's why I love this recipe so much. There's none of that extra work here. Plus, the watermelon/tomato/feta/cucumber combination is bright and fresh (and reliably contrasts with whatever is being charred on the grill, if that's how you'd like to use it) and the ratio of produce is the easy-on-the-brain 1:1:1. It's a good one to have on repeat in July and August.

2 cups diced seedless watermelon (about 12 ounces)

2 cups diced cucumber (about 2 medium cucumbers)

2 cups diced tomatoes (any kind, the sweeter the better)

1 cup crumbled feta cheese (about 4½ ounces)

½ cup chopped fresh mint

⅓ cup extra-virgin olive oil

¼ cup red wine vinegar

Kosher salt and freshly ground black pepper to taste

In a large salad bowl, combine the watermelon, cucumbers, tomatoes, feta, mint, olive oil, vinegar, and salt and pepper. Use your hands to gently toss. Chill as long as you can to allow flavors to meld—up to 12 hours.

Sliced Orange Salad
with Fennel & Shallots

UNDER 30 MINUTES | VEGAN

SERVES 2
(LARGE SERVINGS)
OR 4
(SMALL SERVINGS)

Okay, so oranges: technically not a vegetable, but if you are like me and can't go a day without consuming one between November and March, then your life is about to get markedly better. A traditional Sicilian salad, the combination of sharp and pungent shallots and juicy-sweet orange segments should be high up on a Top 10 best-food-pairings list, and the fennel only adds to that. There is nothing simpler—especially when you forego the fussy supreming for basic cross sections, as I do here. P.S. I'd argue it's elegant enough for a holiday side, with the added benefit of offering a brightness and acidity amid the platters of richer dishes.

2 tablespoons thinly sliced (microscopically thin if possible) shallots

3 tablespoons champagne vinegar

4 navel oranges, peeled and sliced horizontally

⅓ cup sliced fennel from 1 small fennel bulb, shaved as thinly as possible (preferably on a mandoline)

2 tablespoons good-quality extra-virgin olive oil

4 fresh mint leaves, finely chopped

Flaky sea salt

In a small bowl or measuring cup, soak the shallots in the vinegar. Let sit at least 2 minutes. Arrange the orange slices on a platter. Top with the shaved fennel and shallots. Drizzle with the olive oil and the champagne vinegar you used for the shallots. Garnish with mint and sea salt. Pretend you are sitting in a centuries-old hilltop Sicilian village overlooking the Ionian sea.

Crispy Sweet Potatoes
with Lemon-Yogurt Dressing & Dukkah

UNDER 30 MINUTES

SERVES 2
(LARGE SERVINGS)
OR 4
(SMALL SERVINGS)

Honestly, this is substantial enough (and pretty enough) to pass off as a vegetarian main course, especially if you serve it surrounded with herby couscous. (If you like the less sweet Murasaki potatoes better, feel free to swap them in.) Dukkah is an Egyptian spice blend, usually made from a mix of nuts and dried spices like hazelnuts, pistachios, coriander, and sesame and fennel seeds. It used to be hard to find, but now you can find it in better supermarkets and, of course, online. Once you have it in the pantry, you'll want to use it on everything. In a pinch, you can swap in crushed pistachios.

1 cup plain yogurt (any fat content, but I like at least 2%)

2 tablespoons extra-virgin olive oil

2 to 3 tablespoons lemon juice

3 tablespoons snipped fresh chives

Kosher salt and freshly ground black pepper to taste

3 medium sweet potatoes or Murasaki potatoes, peeled and cubed

¼ cup vegetable oil

¼ teaspoon cayenne pepper

1 tablespoon smoked paprika

½ teaspoon garlic powder

¼ cup dukkah or crushed pistachios

1 bunch scallions, white and light-green parts only, finely minced

1 Preheat the oven to 425°F. Line a sheet pan with parchment paper.

2 In a small bowl or 2-cup liquid measuring cup, whisk together the yogurt, olive oil, lemon juice, chives, and some salt and pepper. Set aside.

3 Place the potatoes on the lined sheet pan. Drizzle with the vegetable oil, then sprinkle with the cayenne, smoked paprika, and garlic powder as well as salt and pepper. Using a spoon or your hands, combine everything so all the potatoes are coated.

4 Roast until the potatoes are a deeper golden-brown and crispy around the edges, about 30 minutes, flipping once about halfway through.

5 Pour and spread the yogurt dressing in a shallow bowl, and top with the potatoes. Finish with the dukkah and scallions.

TO VEGANIZE: REPLACE THE YOGURT WITH PLAIN NONDAIRY YOGURT

Crispy Curried Cauliflower
with Coconut & Raisins

QUICK CLEANUP | UNDER 30 MINUTES | VEGAN

For something that comes together so quickly, this combination of heavy-hitter ingredients packs an enormous amount of flavor. To ensure the crispiest cauliflower in the shortest amount of time, cut the stalk into small florets. Madras curry powder is curry powder with a spike of heat—if you don't have it, just add ¼ teaspoon of cayenne to your blend. Note: I make this for at-home lunch—halving the recipe—on the regs.

2 medium heads cauliflower, stems and rough outer leaves removed, and heads chopped into small florets

2 tablespoons Madras curry powder (or milder curry powder plus ¼ teaspoon cayenne)

Kosher salt and freshly ground black pepper to taste

¼ cup extra-virgin olive oil

⅓ cup unsweetened coconut flakes

⅓ cup slivered almonds (whole are fine, roughly chopped, if that's what you have)

Juice from ½ lime

⅓ cup golden raisins

Toppings: nondairy plain yogurt, cilantro, or chives

1   Preheat the oven to 425°F. Line a sheet pan with parchment paper or foil.

2   Spread the cauliflower on the lined pan. Sprinkle with the curry powder and salt and pepper, then drizzle the olive oil all over, using your hands to make sure all the florets are coated.

3   Roast for 30 minutes, stirring halfway through, until the florets are golden and crispy.

4   Remove the sheet pan from the oven, add the coconut flakes and almonds, and use a wooden spoon or long-handled utensil to toss them into the cauliflower while making sure the coconut and almonds are not *buried* by the cauliflower. Return to the oven to roast until both the coconut and almonds look toasted, 5 to 7 minutes. (Keep an eye on them so they don't burn.)

5   Remove the sheet pan from the oven and slide everything into a serving bowl. Squeeze the lime juice all over, then toss in the raisins and serve with desired toppings.

PHOTOGRAPH ON PAGE 45

Quickest Antipasto-Bar Salad

UNDER 30 MINUTES

*SERVES 2
(LARGE SERVINGS)
OR 4
(SMALL SERVINGS)*

This is truly the most no-brainer salad I make and therefore the one I make the most often, mostly because it doesn't require whisking up a dressing. I just use whatever vinegary oil the marinated artichokes and Peppadews are steeping in the jar or at the supermarket salad bar. Done and done.

6 cups baby butter leaf lettuce
(8 to 10 ounces)

1 cup jarred marinated artichokes with marinade

8 to 10 marinated Peppadew peppers

2 tablespoons finely chopped red onion

⅓ cup crumbled feta cheese

⅓ cup finely chopped fresh dill

Juice of ½ lemon

Freshly ground black pepper
to taste

Red wine vinegar
(optional)

In a large salad bowl, toss together the lettuce, artichokes with about ½ cup of the marinade, the Peppadews, onion, feta, dill, lemon juice, and black pepper. If you need more dressing or if the dressing needs more brightness, add a drizzle of vinegar. That's it—I told you it was easy!

TO VEGANIZE: OMIT THE FETA

PHOTOGRAPH ON PAGE 30

Gem Lettuce Salad
WITH Honey-Sea Salt Almonds & Gorgonzola

MAKE-AHEAD (NUTS, DRESSING)

SERVES 4

You can probably tell by all the cheffy "subrecipes" (recipes within recipes) that this salad is based on one I ate at a restaurant—Harper's in Westchester County, New York. I loved the bright yogurt-y take on Green Goddess dressing, the salty-sweet pop from the honey-sea salt almonds, the slight funk from the cheese—and the chef, Chris Vergara, was nice enough to share the recipe with me. But because it involves whirling the Green Goddess dressing (read: breaking out the food processor) and baking a batch of honey-sea salt almonds (read: extra bowl and sheet pan to wash), it was mostly something I made on the weekends, or served to dinner guests on a Saturday night. And you should think of it that way, too. However, should the spirit move you on a weeknight when you are on the clock, you can shave off a significant amount of time by always having a batch of those sweet-and-salty almonds at the ready, and by replacing the dressing with an avocado, then just whisking up a simple dressing like my Champagne Vinaigrette (page 202). No blender required.

6 cups Gem lettuce, 8 to 10 ounces

4 radishes (any kind), thinly sliced

⅓ cup salted roasted sunflower seeds

Kosher salt and freshly ground black pepper to taste

½ cup crumbled Gorgonzola cheese

⅓ cup Honey-Sea Salt Almonds (page 214)

½ cup Spicy Avo Sauce (page 227), **or 1 avocado** (sliced) and **Champagne Vinaigrette** (page 202)

In a large bowl, combine the lettuce, radishes, sunflower seeds, and salt and pepper and gently toss to combine. Add the Gorgonzola and almonds, then gently toss with the dressing right before serving.

TO VEGANIZE: OMIT THE GORGONZOLA AND SWAP IN ROASTED SALTED ALMONDS FOR THE HONEY-SEA SALT ONES

Butter-Fried Cabbage
with Apples

UNDER 30 MINUTES

**SERVES 2
(LARGE BOWLS)
OR 4
(SMALL BOWLS)**

The key here is patience: You have to resist the urge to stir the cabbage. Letting it sear and brown in the pan is how it gets its deep, caramelized flavor. I love this paired with the Homiest Roasted Tomato Soup (page 37).

3 tablespoons unsalted butter

1 small yellow onion, thinly sliced

2 teaspoons sweet paprika

Kosher salt and freshly ground black pepper to taste

½ large head napa cabbage (about 1 pound, 4 ounces), sliced into medium shreds

1 apple (any kind, except Red Delicious), peeled, cored, and cut into small cubes

⅓ cup distilled white vinegar

½ cup chopped fresh dill

¼ cup sour cream or crème fraîche

1 In a large skillet, melt the butter over medium-high heat. Add the onion, paprika, salt, and pepper and cook, stirring occasionally, until the onions are golden, about 5 minutes.

2 Stir in the cabbage and apple and let them cook without stirring so the cabbage can brown and caramelize, about 6 minutes. Then stir once and let sit again without stirring for another 10 minutes, until everything looks golden and toasty. Remove from the heat and stir in the vinegar.

3 Serve garnished with dill and dollops of sour cream.

Avocado-Cucumber Salad
with Carrot-Ginger Dressing & Chives

UNDER 30 MINUTES | VEGAN

SERVES 2 (LARGE BOWLS) OR 4 (SMALL BOWLS)

Like everyone else on earth, my daughters became addicted to the classic bright-orange carrot-ginger dressing from the moment they ordered their first green salad at a favorite local Japanese spot. And I found that when they were young, if I made my own, it was like fairy dust; anything underneath the dressing (greens, steamed broccoli, or green beans) was just a vehicle for its gingery-punchy goodness. But I'd say the way the dressing appears most often in our kitchen is this way—atop creamy avocado and bright, crunchy cucumbers, opposite textures that dance so nicely together. If you're so inclined, you could also top this salad with furikake, the sweet-and-salty seasoning made with crushed nori and sesame seeds, or even just a sprinkle of toasted sesame seeds.

DRESSING

2 tablespoons sweet white miso

2 medium carrots, roughly cut into large pieces

1-inch piece fresh ginger, peeled and roughly chopped

¼ cup neutral oil, such as grapeseed or canola

¼ cup unseasoned rice vinegar

1 tablespoon toasted sesame oil

Kosher salt and freshly ground black pepper to taste

SALAD

1 large avocado, cut into ½-inch chunks

4 to 5 small Japanese cucumbers, cut into ½-inch chunks

⅓ cup snipped fresh chives

Toasted sesame seeds, for serving (optional)

1 **Make the dressing:** In a mini food processor or blender, combine the miso, carrots, ginger, neutral oil, rice vinegar, sesame oil, and salt and pepper. Process until smooth and drizzle-able, about 30 seconds. Add water as necessary to reach a drizzly consistency.

2 **Assemble the salad:** Arrange the avocado and cucumbers on a platter and drizzle about ½ cup of the dressing all over. Sprinkle with the chives and sesame seeds (if using), and serve.

Blasted Artichokes
WITH Yogurt-Dill Dressing

FREEZE IT | UNDER 30 MINUTES | QUICK CLEANUP

SERVES 2
(LARGE BOWLS)
OR 4
(SMALL BOWLS)

This is not something I should probably admit as a so-called professional, but I very rarely pick up fresh artichokes at the market and do the whole carving, de-spiking, and prepping myself. This has especially been the case ever since I discovered frozen bagged artichoke hearts at the supermarket, which you can dump right from the bag onto a hot pan with fantastic, charry results. I often eat them as is for a quick and healthy vegetarian lunch when I'm not partnering them with soup (see pages 34–35) for dinner.

2 tablespoons extra-virgin olive oil

12 ounces frozen halved artichoke hearts (no need to thaw)

½ cup Yogurt-Dill Dressing (page 207)

Lemon wedges, for squeezing

1 Set a cast-iron skillet over medium-high heat and add the oil and artichokes, cut-side down. Let them smoke and steam from the heat contrast but don't touch them for at least 5 minutes. (That is how they will get their char.)

2 At the 5-minute mark, flip an artichoke over to see if it is golden-dark brown. If yes, then turn the heat down to medium and cook, tossing, until warmed through, about another 5 minutes. If no, then give it another minute before peeking again and tossing.

3 Transfer to a serving dish and dollop with the yogurt-dill dressing and serve with lemon wedges.

TO VEGANIZE: USE NONDAIRY YOGURT, SUCH AS KITE HILL ALMOND MILK PLAIN, IN THE DRESSING

One-Pan Spaghetti Squash
WITH Tomatoes & Burrata

QUICK CLEANUP

SERVES 2
(LARGE SERVINGS)
OR 4
(SMALL SERVINGS)

I was never the cook who replaced fettuccine and tagliatelle with zoodles and spaghetti squash—until I discovered this absurdly easy recipe, which I came to think of as a "cold-weather caprese." The juice from the roasted tomatoes join forces with the creamy burrata to create the most luxurious sauce.

1 medium spaghetti squash (about 1½ pounds), halved, seeded, and strings removed

2 cups cherry tomatoes

2 to 3 fresh oregano sprigs

2 tablespoons extra-virgin olive oil

Kosher salt and freshly ground black pepper to taste

2 tablespoons unsalted butter

½ cup grated Pecorino

8 fresh basil leaves, stacked, rolled, and thinly sliced

4 ounces burrata

1 Preheat the oven to 400°F. Line a sheet pan with parchment paper.

2 Place the squash halves cut-side up on the lined pan. Add the tomatoes and oregano sprigs and drizzle the olive oil all over the vegetables, using your fingers to spread the oil on the tomatoes and the exposed flesh of the squash. Season everything with salt and pepper.

3 Roast until the flesh of the squash looks golden around the edges, about 40 minutes.

4 Let the squash rest until it is cool enough to handle (but still warm), then shred the flesh with a fork into a large bowl. (You could also use a potholder to handle the squash if you want to speed things along.)

5 Toss in the butter, pecorino, and some generous grinds of black pepper. Top the squash with the roasted tomatoes, basil, and the burrata, breaking up the cheese with your fingers to allow the creamy interior to ooze and distribute across the vegetables.

TO VEGANIZE: REPLACE THE BUTTER WITH OLIVE OIL AND OMIT THE PECORINO AND BURRATA

Pomegranate-Glazed Eggplant
WITH Whipped Feta

MAKE-AHEAD

SERVES 4

I feel like any recipe that combines pomegranates with eggplant should be legally required to credit Yotam Ottolenghi, the Israeli-born British superstar chef, as inspiration. The cover of his seminal 2010 cookbook *Plenty* (and every other page inside its cover) proved that vegetables—particularly charred, creamy eggplants studded with jewel-like pomegranate seeds—could be elevated to an art form. I will never tire of that combination, and here, I up the ante, using pomegranate molasses for an extra sweet-tart hit. When I'm feeling fancy, I bring this to potlucks—whipped feta is, in general, a guaranteed crowd-pleaser. If you don't have time to make whipped feta, you can also serve the eggplant on a bed of plain yogurt.

1 large eggplant, sliced into ¼-inch-thick rounds and then halved

2 tablespoons pomegranate molasses

1 tablespoon white wine vinegar

3 tablespoons extra-virgin olive oil, plus more for brushing and drizzling

Kosher salt and freshly ground black pepper to taste

Whipped Feta (page 231) **or plain yogurt**

Fresh mint, finely chopped

Pomegranate seeds (optional)

1 Preheat the oven to 425°F. Line a sheet pan with parchment paper.

2 Spread the eggplant slices in a baking dish in a single layer. In a measuring cup, whisk together the pomegranate molasses, vinegar, olive oil, and salt and pepper. Pour on top of the eggplant and flip the pieces around so each one absorbs the marinade. Let sit for 10 minutes and then flip again. (You can also do this in a zip-top bag. Just re-use the bag so it's not a single-use situation.) After about 15 minutes of marinating, place the eggplant rounds on the lined sheet pan.

3 Bake for 15 minutes. Flip each round over with a fork, brush on a little more olive oil, and bake until golden and crispy (as shown), another 15 minutes.

4 Arrange the eggplant on top of the whipped feta (as shown, overlapping slightly), then top with the fresh mint, pomegranate seeds (if using), freshly ground black pepper, and a drizzle of olive oil.

Sliced Avocado Salad
WITH Arugula & Crispy Capers

MAKE-AHEAD | UNDER 30 MINUTES

SERVES 2
(LARGE BOWLS)
OR 4
(SMALL BOWLS)

I love how each ingredient here brings so much to the final dish: The peppery arugula, the creamy avocado, the bright briny pop of the crispy-fried capers. You can get everything ready ahead of time for this except the avocados, which are the main event here, obviously. (That's why there are 3 of them for 4 servings.) Slice them at the last minute to avoid oxidizing, i.e., browning.

Crispy Capers
(page 223)

DRESSING

¼ cup fresh
lemon juice
(about 1½ lemons)

1½ teaspoons Dijon
mustard

1½ teaspoons
honey

Kosher salt and
freshly ground
black pepper
to taste

⅓ cup extra-virgin
olive oil

SALAD

4 cups arugula, or
3 cups arugula plus
1 cup sprouts (any
kind)

3 avocados,
sliced horizontally
as shown

3 tablespoons
minced red onion
or shallots

¼ cup chopped
fresh parsley

Flaky sea salt and
freshly ground
black pepper

1 Make the crispy capers, if you haven't already.

2 Make the dressing: In a small bowl or screw-top jar, combine the lemon juice, mustard, honey, salt and pepper, and olive oil. Whisk or cover and shake until emulsified.

3 Assemble the salad: Add the arugula (but not the sprouts, if using) to a wide shallow bowl or a deep platter and top with the avocado slices. Add the minced onion and parsley, then drizzle the dressing all over. Top with the sprouts (if using), crispy capers, and finish with a pinch of sea salt (not a lot! capers are salty!) and a few grinds of black pepper.

*TO VEGANIZE: SWAP IN SUGAR FOR THE
HONEY IN THE DRESSING*

Sugar Snap Pea Salad
TWO WAYS

MAKE-AHEAD | UNDER 30 MINUTES | VEGAN

**SERVES 2
(LARGE BOWLS)
OR 4
(SMALL BOWLS)**

When sugar snap peas are in season they are pretty much always on my plate in some form, but these two forms are my favorite. On nights when I want my salad to have a little heft, I make the peanutty version. But when I'm relying on it to bring brightness to the plate and my palate, I go with arugula-pesto.

9 ounces sugar snap peas (about 2½ cups), ends trimmed and sliced thinly on a diagonal

1 medium radish, sliced as thinly as you can manage

12 fresh mint leaves, finely chopped

SPICY PEANUT

¼ cup salted roasted peanuts, crushed or chopped

3 tablespoons Peanut-Lime Dressing (page 205)

Kosher salt and freshly ground black pepper to taste

ARUGULA PESTO

½ cup Arugula Pesto (page 229)

Kosher salt and freshly ground black pepper to taste

In a medium bowl, combine the snap peas, radish, and mint.

For the SPICY PEANUT Version: Add the crushed peanuts, toss with the peanut dressing, and season to taste with salt and pepper.

For the ARUGULA PESTO Version: Toss with the arugula pesto and season with salt and pepper to taste.

PHOTOGRAPH ON PAGE 51

Choose-Your-Own-Adventure Slaw

MAKE-AHEAD | UNDER 30 MINUTES

SERVES 4 This recipe is what I consider my go-to, the slaw that appears most often next to potato salads and grilled goodies in the summer, but I encourage you to swap in any of the dressings in the Hooks chapter—e.g., maybe Yogurt-Dill Dressing (page 207), for a light and fresher slaw? Or Ginger-Miso Dressing (page 211) when you're craving Asian flavors? It's hard to go wrong.

6 cups shredded green cabbage (from ½ medium head)

1 small carrot (optional; I like it for color), shaved with a vegetable peeler

3 tablespoons finely chopped fresh dill

1 tablespoon finely minced red onion or shallot

Kosher salt and freshly ground black pepper to taste

DRESSING

¼ cup apple cider vinegar

2 tablespoons mayonnaise or plain yogurt

1½ teaspoons Dijon mustard

¼ teaspoon sugar

1 teaspoon celery seeds (optional)

Kosher salt and freshly ground black pepper to taste

⅓ cup extra-virgin olive oil

1 In a large bowl, combine the cabbage, carrot (if using), dill, red onion, and salt and pepper.

2 Make the dressing: In a jar or measuring cup, whisk together the vinegar, mayonnaise, mustard, sugar, celery seeds (if using), salt and pepper, and olive oil. Whisk or cover and shake until emulsified.

3 Toss the cabbage mixture with the dressing until well coated.

Roasted Vegetables
with Miso Butter

UNDER 30 MINUTES

I learned this miso-butter trick from Kay Chun, a recipe developer for the *New York Times*, and an old co-worker from *Real Simple* magazine, where in our early days, we both obsessed over how to make recipes easier and faster. (This one would've been a hall of famer.) It simply involves smashing together two MVP ingredients, in this case, miso and butter, along with a few aromatics, then tossing the flavor-bomb result with almost any roasted vegetable you fancy. If you want to roast a few different kinds of vegetables, use the chart below to see which ones have similar roasting times. You can also reserve room on the sheet pan and add quicker-roasting vegetables as you go.

6 tablespoons unsalted butter, at room temperature

2 tablespoons sweet white miso

Flaky sea salt

Aromatics: 1 garlic clove, pressed, *or* **1-inch fresh ginger, peeled and grated,** *or* **2 scallions, white and light green parts only,** minced

Vegetable or vegetable combination of your choice (see list below)

Extra-virgin olive oil

QUICK ROAST (15–20 MINUTES)
Asparagus, Tomatoes (whole cherry or halved Romas), **Onions** (any kind), **Broccoli** (small florets), **Cauliflower** (small florets)

MEDIUM ROAST (25–30 MINUTES)
Brussels Sprouts (halved), **Carrots, Mushrooms**

LONGER ROAST (30–40 MINUTES)
Beets, Butternut Squash, Potatoes, Eggplant (make sure you line your sheet pan with parchment paper, not foil)

1 In a small bowl, mash the butter, miso, a pinch of sea salt, and desired aromatic (or aromatics) together. Store the miso butter in the refrigerator until you are ready to use. (It keeps up to 1 month.)

2 Preheat the oven to 425°F. Line a sheet pan with parchment paper or foil. If you are mixing vegetables with different roasting times (quick roast, medium roast, longer roast), use a separate sheet for each category so you can easily remove from the oven once they are respectively roasted and tender.

3 Cut your chosen vegetables into bite-size pieces and toss them with enough olive oil to lightly coat, not drench. Roast until the vegetables reach golden crisp-tenderness, according to the list at left.

4 After the vegetables have finished roasting, slide them into a serving dish or bowl, then add a tablespoon of the miso butter for approximately every cup of vegetables. Stir and serve warm.

MISO BUTTER: CONSIDER ALL YOUR
ROASTED VEGETABLES MAJORLY
UPGRADED

YOUR NEW FAVORITE WAY TO EAT
EGGS FOR DINNER (PAGE 83)

Skillet

&

Sheet Pan Dinners

OR

Who says Vegetarian Cooking has to be Complicated?

Recipes

AT SOME POINT IN MY VEGETARIAN COOKING CAREER, most likely after a "small plates night" when I'd wind up using every platter and small appliance in my kitchen to make a variety of mix-and-match dishes for a restaurant-like experience, I became very mindful about how much cooking gear was involved in getting a vegetable-forward meal on the table: Why use the wooden spoon to stir the eggs and a serving spoon to scoop them, when I can easily get away with just one of those? Why break out separate measuring cups for adding ingredients to a bowl, when I can just use a large 4-cup glass measuring cup to be all things, including the mixing bowl? Why use serving platters on a regular old Tuesday night, when it's eminently possible to create a welcoming dinner table with place mats and linens, while asking your diners to go ahead and get seconds from the stovetop.

There are some nights when I don't mind using all the gear, when time allows for more involved kinds of cleaning... I mean cooking. But if it's a weeknight and I'm donning my gear-minimizing goggles, I opt for one of these skillet dinners. Almost all of them rely on using (and cleaning) only one big-ticket item. Excluding the goggles.

Menemen (Turkish Scrambled Eggs *with* Tomatoes & Spices)

QUICK CLEANUP | UNDER 30 MINUTES

SERVES 4

After my father-in-law died, we moved my mother-in-law, Emily, up to New York from Virginia, where she had lived for almost fifty years, so she could be closer to her kids and grandkids. I don't want to say it was easy, but it is really great for her to be only twenty minutes away from us now as opposed to five hours. One of our new rituals became Sunday lunch, and we almost always go to the same little Turkish spot, the next town over from her new apartment. Emily and Steve, my father-in-law, lived in Ankara in the 1970s, when Steve was in the foreign service, and Emily loves to remind the restaurant's owner of this fact whenever he seats us. As for me, I've come to really look forward to one dish on their menu listed as Turkish Scrambled Eggs, which I later found out was called menemen, and is one of the country's most popular comfort foods. It's simply soft scrambled eggs tossed with onions and tomatoes and spiked with paprika or Urfa pepper, which lends it a uniquely sweet depth. I am always in search of techniques that "dinner-fy" scrambled eggs, and I took to this method immediately. You can find Urfa biber—made from the distinctively dark colored chile pepper found in the southern part of Turkey—at any specialty store or online, and use it anywhere you'd use black pepper; on roasted vegetables, for instance. I usually serve menemen with a green salad and warmed pita.

3 tablespoons extra-virgin olive oil

1 medium yellow onion, finely diced

3 tablespoons finely chopped green bell pepper

1 teaspoon Urfa biber (or hot paprika, but try to find Urfa biber)

¼ teaspoon cayenne pepper

Kosher salt and freshly ground black pepper to taste

1 (15-ounce) can (or 1½ cups) diced tomatoes

7 large eggs, whisked

Flatbread or pita, for serving

1 In a large nonstick or cast-iron skillet, heat the olive oil over medium-low heat. Add the onion, green pepper, Urfa biber, cayenne, and salt and pepper and cook, stirring occasionally, until the onions are cooked down, about 6 minutes.

2 Stir in the tomatoes and cook until warmed through, another 5 minutes. Scoop out one cup of the vegetables and set aside to cool a little. To the remaining vegetables in the pan, add the eggs and stir until the eggs are just barely set. (Traditional menemen calls for scrambling the eggs *very* gently just until set.) Turn off the heat and stir in the reserved vegetables.

3 Serve immediately with warmed bread for scooping.

Spicy Feta Chickpea Wedges
WITH Arugula Pesto

MAKE-AHEAD | QUICK CLEANUP

SERVES 4

I once made these for a friend who is gluten-free and I'll never forget what she told me—after catching her breath from inhaling them so quickly. She said something to the effect of "Don't get me wrong, I love salads and vegetables, but it's so awesome when someone serves me a delicious gluten-free carb." These crispy flavorful wedges, based on socca, the Provençal street food, are made with chickpea flour (aka besan if you buy it from an Indian market), and in addition to being an indulgent carb to make for the appreciative gluten-free set, they are protein *packed*. When the kids were little, I'd make chickpea fries and serve them with a basic marinara as a dip—like French fries and ketchup, but with a PhD. Here, I give them the main-course treatment, slicing the uncooked and chilled pancake into pizza-like wedges, then frying them in olive oil, finishing with a generous drizzle of arugula pesto, and topping with sprouts.

Kosher salt

1 tablespoon plus ¼ cup extra-virgin olive oil

1½ cups chickpea flour

3 ounces feta cheese, crumbled into small pieces

1 teaspoon ground cumin

1 teaspoon smoked paprika

½ teaspoon garlic powder

¼ teaspoon cayenne, or more to taste

Sprouts (optional), for serving

Arugula Pesto (page 229)

TO VEGANIZE: OMIT THE FETA

1 Lay a piece of parchment paper on a largeish cutting board (one that can fit into your refrigerator) and set aside. In a heavy medium saucepan, bring 3 cups of salted water to a boil.

2 Add 1 tablespoon of the oil to the water and reduce the heat to medium-low. Add the chickpea flour in a steady stream, whisking constantly for about 3 minutes. The batter will become thick and begin to pull away from the sides of the pan, like polenta. Remove from the heat, fold in the feta with a silicone spatula, and transfer the batter to the parchment paper, using the spatula to spread it evenly and quickly so it forms a thick round shape with the thickness of steak fries or a frittata. The batter will begin to firm up right away. Let cool slightly at room temperature, then refrigerate for at least 30 minutes, uncovered. (If you chill it for longer than 30 minutes, cover with foil, and then let it sit at room temperature for 15 minutes before frying.)

3 While the batter is chilling, in a small bowl, combine 1 teaspoon salt, the cumin, smoked paprika, garlic powder, and cayenne. Set the spice mixture aside.

4 Remove the chilled round from the fridge and cut into 8 wedges like a pie (as shown on page 87) on the cutting board.

5 Line a plate with paper towels and set near the stove. Have the bowl of spice mixture nearby, too. In a large skillet, preferably cast-iron, heat the remaining ¼ cup olive oil over medium-high heat. Add 6 or so wedges to the olive oil (don't crowd the pan) and fry for 2 to 3 minutes per side, flipping with a spatula when golden. Transfer the wedges to the paper towels to drain and season with the desired amount of spice mixture. Repeat with the remaining wedges.

6 Serve warm if possible, topped with sprouts (if using), and drizzled with arugula pesto.

SPICY FETA CHICKPEA WEDGES
WITH ARUGULA PESTO
(PAGE 84)

Buckwheat Crepes *WITH* Goat Cheese, Asparagus & Mushrooms

QUICK CLEANUP | UNDER 30 MINUTES

MAKES 4 LARGE CREPES (SERVES 4)

Pre-pandemic, our breakfasts were mostly on-the-go affairs. Maybe a banana grabbed while sprinting through the kitchen, backpack already slung over shoulders, or, if we were feeling fancy, peanut butter on toast. Post March 2020, breakfast became a whole new ball game, and probably like many of you, after working through the confusion and fear, we turned to the kitchen for comfort and joy. And when I say joy, I specifically mean crepes, because what makes a regular old Tuesday morning feel more special than walking into the kitchen to see my daughter spreading Nutella on a delicate eggy pancake, dotted with strawberries and showered in powdered sugar? That was the breakfast crepe. Lunch was ham and cheese, dessert was lemon and powdered sugar. We made them so often I memorized the recipe.

It wasn't until a few years later, when the girls had left for college and the world was out and about again, that I pulled out the recipe, this time swapping in buckwheat flour for a third of the all-purpose, in order to make crepes feel more like a capital-D Dinner. And you know what I discovered? Even though crepes feel kind of fancy for breakfast, they are actually a quick-and-easy dinner, and way kinder to a cook than you might think. Plus, buckwheat lends an excellent nuttiness to crepes, especially when contrasted with tangy-sweet honeyed goat cheese folded inside. You don't have to be too faithful to the asparagus-mushroom combination here. Feel free to substitute whatever is in season along with a cheese to match. P.S. You can pick up store-bought (nonbuckwheat) crepes at most supermarkets now, which will definitely fast-track the whole operation. Also, if you don't have buckwheat flour, you can just swap it out for equal parts all-purpose.

VEGETABLES

12 ounces mushrooms (any kind, I like shiitakes or cremini), sliced

2 pounds asparagus, woody ends trimmed, chopped into largeish pieces, as shown

½ medium yellow onion, 1 leek, or 1 shallot, roughly chopped

¼ cup extra-virgin olive oil

Kosher salt and freshly ground black pepper to taste

3 ounces honey goat cheese (or regular goat cheese plus a drizzle of honey)

1 teaspoon chili crisp, or more to taste

CREPE BATTER

1 cup ice water

½ cup milk (any kind, but preferably whole)

2 large eggs

4 tablespoons unsalted butter, melted, plus more (up to 2 to 3 tablespoons) for the pan

½ teaspoon kosher salt

½ cup all-purpose flour

⅓ cup buckwheat flour

(continued on page 90)

1 Roast the vegetables: Preheat the oven to 425°F. Line a sheet pan with parchment paper.

2 Spread the mushrooms, asparagus, and onion on the lined sheet pan. Toss the vegetables with the olive oil and salt and pepper and roast until the vegetables are crispy around the edges, about 25 minutes.

3 Remove from the oven and, fashioning a "chute" out of the parchment paper, slide the vegetables into a bowl. Toss with dots of goat cheese and chili crisp until the cheese has melted somewhat.

4 Meanwhile, make the crepe batter: In a large bowl, whisk together the ice water, milk, eggs, and melted butter. Add the salt and both the all-purpose and buckwheat flours and whisk until smooth and combined.

5 Heat a nonstick medium skillet over medium heat. Add a pat of butter to the skillet. When it's melted and gets a little brown, add ⅓ cup of batter to the skillet, tilting the skillet around, so the batter covers the surface in as thin a layer as possible. Once tiny bubbles appear, after about 1 minute, flip and cook another minute or so, until the crepe is cooked through and looks speckly golden-brown as shown.

6 Slide onto a large platter, heap a thin layer of mushroom-asparagus mixture on top, and fold as shown or just roll enchilada style. Tent with foil to keep warm, and repeat with the remaining batter and filling, adding butter to the pan as you go.

CREPES ALL YEAR LONG: TRY THESE VEGETABLE COMBINATIONS THROUGH THE SEASONS

SPRING
- **Steamed spinach + goat cheese + chives**
- **Mushrooms + Gruyère + thyme**

SUMMER
- **Roasted bell peppers (red, yellow, orange) + feta + thyme**
- **Roasted cherry tomatoes + raw corn kernels + ricotta + basil**

FALL
- **Roasted butternut squash + red chiles + feta**
- **Sautéed shredded Brussels sprouts + Boursin**

WINTER
- **Skillet-caramelized cabbage and onions + Parmesan**
- **Roasted broccoli + cheddar**

Shredded Zucchini & Basil Frittata
WITH Potatoes
(AKA ANDY'S FRITTATA)

QUICK CLEANUP | UNDER 30 MINUTES

SERVES 4

If you're like the old me, you probably have some version of a frittata in your vegetarian dinner repertoire, but just sort of wing it every time—whether that's with ingredients or technique. And, of course, therein lies the beauty of a frittata, which wraps the egg and potato component of your favorite hearty breakfast into one easy-to-cook minimal mess dinner package. But the new me would like to introduce you to my husband's frittata. Andy taught me to cut the potatoes into a very small dice, which allows me to skip the parboiling step (and parboiling pot). And instead of baking it low and slow like some recipes advise, he broils it at the end for only a few minutes, and it still gets nice and puffy while the eggs retain their tenderness. All in all, it's a winner, especially with this summery combination of zucchini and basil.

3 tablespoons extra-virgin olive oil

12 ounces potatoes (about 3 small Yukon Gold or red potatoes), peeled and cut into very tiny dice

Kosher salt and freshly ground pepper to taste

Red pepper flakes to taste

½ yellow onion, finely chopped

1 large zucchini (12 ounces), shredded and squeezed dry in a kitchen towel (see page 93)

8 large eggs, whisked

½ cup whole milk

1 cup grated Gruyère or Italian Fontina cheese

½ cup freshly grated Parmesan cheese

Fresh basil, stacked, rolled, and thinly sliced (for serving)

1 Arrange an oven rack in the middle of the oven and heat the broiler. Add the olive oil to a 9-inch cast-iron or other broilerproof skillet and set over medium-high heat. Add the potatoes in one layer (as much as possible), season with salt and pepper, and let sit without stirring. After 3 minutes of sizzling, use a wooden spoon to scrape them off the bottom of the pan and toss (this helps keep those brown crispy parts on the potato). Continue to cook, stirring occasionally, until the potatoes are golden and brown on most sides, about 6 minutes total.

(continued on next page)

THE SQUEEZE: EASIEST WAY TO EXTRACT
MOISTURE FROM YOUR ZUCCHINI

2 Stir in some red pepper flakes and the onion and cook until softened, 2 to 3 minutes. Add the zucchini and cook until wilted, another 3 minutes. In a bowl, whisk together the eggs, milk, Gruyère, and ¼ cup of the Parmesan. Pour this mixture over the potatoes evenly, stirring a little (or poking through the vegetables) to allow the eggs to seep down to the bottom of the pan. Let sit without stirring for 4 to 5 minutes, until the eggs look cooked around the edges.

3 Sprinkle the remaining ¼ cup Parmesan on top and place the skillet under the broiler for about 2 minutes, until the eggs are cooked and slightly puffy, and the cheese looks melted. (Keep an eye on it to make sure it doesn't burn.) Remove and cool slightly.

4 Using a silicone spatula, loosen the frittata around the edges of the pan, then slice into wedges and serve topped with the basil.

Abby's Brilliant Beans 'n' Cheese

QUICK CLEANUP

SERVES 4

A few years ago, my daughter Abby walked into the kitchen, saw a pot of beans on the stove and said, "You know what would be really good? If you made beans the way you make mac and cheese." And she was right. Partly. Because here's the beauty of this dinner: The whole béchamel thing that is usually so crucial to making mac and cheese? I skipped that part. The cream? Skipped that, too. The multiple pots and pans? Nope! This meal is cooked in one pot. Its relation to mac and cheese lies mostly in the crunchy topping and the peppery cheeses mixed in with the beans. Brilliant.

6 tablespoons extra-virgin olive oil

1 medium onion, chopped

Pinch of red pepper flakes

Kosher salt

25 meaningful grinds of black pepper

2 garlic cloves, peeled and minced

1 tablespoon dried mustard powder

4½ cups cooked white beans, such as Great Northern or cannellini, or 3 (15-ounce) cans, rinsed (you want them to be a little wet)

1 cup (about 2¾ ounces) shredded Gruyère cheese

1 cup (about 2¾ ounces) shredded sharp cheddar cheese

1 cup panko bread crumbs

3 tablespoons freshly grated Parmesan cheese

Leaves from 3 or 4 fresh thyme sprigs

1   In a large deep broilerproof skillet, heat 3 tablespoons of the olive oil over medium heat. Add the onion, pepper flakes, and salt and black pepper. Cook, stirring occasionally, until the onion has softened, about 5 minutes. Add the garlic and mustard powder. Cook for 1 minute.

2   Add the beans to the pan (the slightly wet beans will help loosen everything) and cook until warmed through, about 5 minutes. Reduce the heat to medium-low, add the Gruyère and cheddar, and stir until melted.

3   Remove from the heat. Arrange an oven rack in the middle of the oven and set the oven to broil. In a medium bowl, mix together the panko with the Parm, remaining 3 tablespoons olive oil, and more salt and black pepper. You want all the panko crumbs to be damp. Using your hands, top the beans with the panko mixture. It might feel like a lot of topping, but persevere. You're going to want the crunch. Place the whole thing in the oven and broil for 1 to 2 minutes, keeping an eye on it the entire time. It's ready when the topping looks golden and toasty. Serve warm, garnished with thyme leaves.

NOTE: I serve this with a chopped tomato salad—3 to 4 cups of chopped cherry tomatoes with basil, olive oil, red wine vinegar, and minced red onion—but any simple green salad (and maybe even a piece of crusty bread) would be just fine.

Roasted Whole Leeks
WITH **Poached Eggs & Chives**

QUICK CLEANUP

I've been threatening to write a cookbook called *I Could Eat This Every Night*, which is what Andy says when I make a very specific kind of dinner, namely something fresh, fast, and without a lot of bells and whistles. This braised leeks dinner, which we've been making a lot since becoming empty nesters, would likely be the first recipe in the book, if not the cover, given how beautiful it looks. When leeks are braised, they become meltingly tender almost, dare I say, meaty. It goes without saying that this dinner will be best in the spring, when you can get your hands on fresh aromatic leeks from the farmers' market. We usually top with poached eggs, but if that is too fussy for you on a weeknight, sunny-side up or over easy are just fine, too—you just really want those runny golden yolks to mingle with the rest of the pan juices to create a silky, indulgent sauce.

4 tablespoons extra-virgin olive oil

½ cup plain bread crumbs

Kosher salt and freshly ground black pepper to taste

4 leeks, white and light-green parts only, trimmed, halved lengthwise as shown, and rinsed (see Note on page 98)

½ cup vegetable broth

1 teaspoon distilled white vinegar

4 large eggs (or however many per person you think you need)

2 tablespoons simple vinaigrette (such as Champagne Vinaigrette, page 202)

Freshly grated pecorino or Parmesan cheese, for serving

Snipped fresh chives and crusty bread, for serving

1   Preheat the oven to 375°F.

2   In a large ovenproof skillet, heat 2 tablespoons of the oil over medium-high heat. Add the bread crumbs in a single layer, season with salt and pepper, and cook without disturbing for 2 minutes. When the bread crumbs start to deepen in color, stir, then once they look crispy and toasty, remove to a small bowl.

3   Wipe down the skillet and place it back over medium-high heat. Add the remaining 2 tablespoons oil, the leeks, cut-side down, and salt and pepper, nestling them tight if you have to. (They'll shrink.) Cook for 5 minutes, flipping halfway through once they are golden brown, to get them a little brown on the second side.

(continued on next page)

4   Pour in the broth and transfer the skillet to the oven. Roast until they're golden and tender (a knife will easily slide through them), about 30 minutes.

5   Line a plate with paper towels and set near the stove. Bring a medium-large pot (big enough for 4 eggs to spread out in a single layer) of water to a boil, then reduce to a very low, steady simmer. (It should be *barely* simmering.) Add the vinegar (this helps the eggs hold their shape). Crack all of the eggs into a medium bowl and slide them into the water all at once. Cook just until the whites look set, about 3 minutes. (You can scoop one out with a slotted spoon

to get a better look. The yolk should be soft to the touch with the white opaque.) Remove them all with a slotted spoon to the paper towels to drain.

6   Divide the leeks evenly between two plates, drizzle with a scant tablespoon of vinaigrette, place 2 eggs on top, then sprinkle with the toasted bread crumbs, pecorino, and chives. Serve with crusty bread.

NOTE: To clean the leeks, rinse them after halving. Run the cut-side under water and, using your hands, gently shift the leek's layers to let the water rinse through.

Sheet Pan Cauliflower & Chickpeas
WITH Creamy Chile-Lime Sauce

QUICK CLEANUP

SERVES 4

The best kind of sheet pan dinner follows a very specific formula: Throw a bunch of things tossed in olive oil onto a sheet pan, then, while it bakes, make a drizzle sauce. Preferably a drizzle sauce that packs a *lot* of flavor. This recipe is exactly that, capitalizing on winter pantry staples and the big bang of jarred chili garlic sauce. You could serve this with rice if you think someone at the table will appreciate it.

1 large head cauliflower, cut into small florets

3 cups cooked chickpeas or 2 (15-ounce) cans, drained and rinsed, dried as much as possible

1 small yellow onion, roughly chopped

½ teaspoon red pepper flakes

Kosher salt and freshly ground black pepper to taste

½ cup extra-virgin olive oil

CHILE-LIME SAUCE

1½ tablespoons chili garlic sauce (I like Huy Fong brand, the one with the rooster logo)

2 tablespoons fresh lime juice

2 tablespoons sour cream

¼ cup neutral oil, such as grapeseed or vegetable

TO FINISH

½ cup roasted salted cashews

Chopped fresh chives, for serving

1 Preheat the oven to 425°F.

2 Add the cauliflower, chickpeas, and onion to a large sheet pan. Sprinkle with the pepper flakes, season with salt and pepper, and drizzle the olive oil all over. Using your hands, mix everything together, making sure every piece is coated with a sheen of oil. (The sheet pan might look crowded, but the cauliflower will shrink as it bakes.)

3 Bake for 45 minutes, stirring with a wooden spoon halfway through. After 45 minutes, stir it again, turn the heat to a high broil, and broil until there is some golden crispiness on the tips of the cauliflower, about 5 minutes. Remove and let cool slightly.

4 **Meanwhile, make the chile-lime sauce:** In a small bowl or screw-top jar, whisk or shake together the chili-garlic sauce, lime juice, sour cream, neutral oil, and 2 tablespoons water.

5 **To finish:** Toss the cashews into the cauliflower-chickpea mixture. Scoop into bowls. Drizzle with the chile-lime sauce and sprinkle with the chives.

Sheet Pan Gnocchi *with* Butternut Squash

QUICK CLEANUP

SERVES 4

I believe this dinner holds the honor of easiest recipe in the book. One pan, minimal ingredients, and almost no chopping if you decide to go with the already peeled and chopped squash you can find in most supermarkets these days. But don't let that fool you into thinking it's boring—I will never get tired of the way gnocchi browns up in the oven, a delightful bounty of crispy little golden biscuits. Add the sweet squash, a little smokiness from the paprika, and you've got yourself a keeper.

1 medium (about 20 ounces) butternut squash, peeled and cut into 1-inch pieces (or prechopped)

1 medium or ½ large yellow onion, chopped

1½ pounds shelf-stable store-bought gnocchi (see Note)

⅓ cup extra-virgin olive oil

2 teaspoons smoked paprika

Kosher salt and freshly ground black pepper to taste

For topping: fresh thyme leaves and fresh ricotta or goat cheese (for dolloping) or **grated ricotta salata**

 TO VEGANIZE: OMIT THE CHEESE AT SERVING

1 Preheat the oven to 425°F.

2 Add the squash and onion to one side of a sheet pan and the gnocchi to the other. (It's okay if it's a little crowded.) Drizzle the olive oil all over and sprinkle on the smoked paprika and salt and pepper. Use your hands to mix the components around (keep the gnocchi and vegetables separate) so every piece is lightly coated. Roast until the squash is golden and cooked through, 30 to 35 minutes, stirring once about halfway through (still keeping the gnocchi and vegetables separate). Slide the oven rack out and scoop the squash off the sheet pan into a serving bowl. Spread out the gnocchi to give each piece a little more room, turn on the broiler, and broil until the gnocchi are browned and crisp all over, 3 to 5 minutes. Remove from the oven and toss with the vegetables.

3 Serve topped with the thyme and cheese of choice.

NOTE: It is well documented that I'm a big fan of Trader Joe's cauliflower gnocchi, but I'd advise avoiding it in this recipe—the gnocchi just don't sufficiently crisp. Best to stick with the traditional flour-and-potato shelf-stable kind. If the cauliflower kind is all you have, please see: Crispy Pan-Fried Gnocchi with Peas & Chiles on page 163.

MUSHROOM-CHARD
BREAD PUDDING
(PAGE 110)

Hearty Comfort Food

OR

How to convince athletes, ravenous teenagers, and the proverbial meat and potatoes eater that vegetarian food is filling

Recipes

WHAT DO THE FOLLOWING PEOPLE HAVE IN COMMON? Alex Morgan, Venus Williams, Novak Djokovic, Chris Paul, Scott Jurek . . . I could go on, but in the interest of getting dinner on the table, I'll stop because I know you know the answer: Yes, they are all megasuccessful athletes. But guess what else? *They are all vegetarians* or *mostly* vegetarians, or in a few cases, vegan.

I start this chapter with that little bit of trivia because I'd like to put to bed the myth that vegetarian food is bird food, food that isn't satisfying, food that doesn't give the super-active, the growing-in-front-of-our-eyes diner (or Olympian!) sufficient fuel for baseball practice, or getting through a day of high school (even a junior-year day of high school!), or a Grand Slam match, or a World Cup final, or in Jurek's case, an ultramarathon. (!!!!).

In this chapter, you'll find large-format center-of-the-table comfort food, the kind of dishes that work when you need a substantial dish to satisfy a ravenous athlete or to act as a main for a vegetarian dinner guest as well as an indulgent side for a meat-eater. When one of these is on the menu, you never have to worry about your team feeling unsatisfied . . . or missing the meat.

Roasted Tomato Tart
with Really Good Blue Cheese

QUICK CLEANUP | UNDER 30 MINUTES

SERVES 2 OR 3 (AS A MAIN) OR 4 (AS A SIDE)

Puff pastry was intimidating to me for the longest time, and I'm not really sure why that is. The most complicated part about baking with it is making sure it's fully thawed in the first place. Once it is, you can roll the pastry a bit thinner, prick it a few times with a fork, top with vegetables, cheese, herbs, and then bake it into the most beautiful tart.

Those instructions are deliberately vague to emphasize how flexible this kind of recipe is—use any vegetable, any cheese, and any herb, and you've got a guaranteed winner. I will say, though, that the winner of winners—the cover girl of winners—in my humble opinion, is this combination of deep red tomatoes and blue cheese, particularly if you've managed to score really good blue cheese like Point Reyes Original Blue or Jasper Hill's Bayley Hazen. (But any blue cheese will work.) Lastly: This can be made ahead of time and served at room temperature.

All-purpose flour, for dusting

1 (14-ounce) package frozen puff pastry, such as all-butter Dufour brand, completely thawed

3 tablespoons extra-virgin olive oil

4 or 5 tomatoes (any kind, but preferably Cherokee Purple or Black Krim, or any deep-dark red heirloom variety), sliced on a cutting board (important, see Note)

3 ounces blue cheese

Kosher salt and freshly ground black pepper to taste

Snipped fresh chives, for garnish

1 Preheat the oven to 400°F.

2 Lightly flour a sheet of parchment paper and roll out the puff pastry on top. Prick the pastry in a few places with a fork and brush all over with 2 tablespoons of the olive oil. Slide the parchment paper onto a sheet pan.

3 Arrange the tomatoes on top (a little overlap is fine, just leave about a 1-inch border), drizzle with the remaining tablespoon of olive oil. (I use my fingers to sort of "paint" the tomatoes.) Then sprinkle with the blue cheese, tucking under the tomatoes here and there, and season with salt and pepper.

4 Bake the tart until the tomatoes look shriveled and the edges of the pastry are browned, puffed, and crisp, 20 to 25 minutes. (Start checking on it after 15 minutes.) Let the tart cool for about 10 minutes, then garnish with the chives and more salt and pepper before slicing and serving.

NOTE: If the tomatoes are super juicy, poke out some of the seeds and pulp while you slice them, which will help prevent dough sogginess. Save the juicy pulp to brush onto Grilled Bread (page 221) to make a pan con tomate.

Mushroom-Chard Bread Pudding

MAKE-AHEAD

SERVES 6 TO 8

This isn't necessarily a quick-and-easy weeknight dinner, but on those nights when, say, book club is coming over, or the mercury has dropped significantly, or you are lucky enough to have a good loaf of bread that's gone stale (yes, *lucky*!), this is the place your brain should go. It's best served with simple greens tossed in a bracing vinaigrette (like Champagne Vinaigrette, page 202).

3 tablespoons extra-virgin olive oil, plus more as needed

8 ounces mushrooms (any kind, I like cremini or shiitake), sliced

1 large yellow onion, roughly chopped

Pinch of red pepper flakes

Kosher salt and freshly ground black pepper to taste

4 cups roughly chopped chard leaves and stems (from about 5 leaves)

3 tablespoons unsalted butter

1 tablespoon mushroom powder (see Note)

2 cups whole milk

1 tablespoon prepared horseradish

Softened butter, for the baking dish

6 cups cubed eggy bread, such as challah, preferably a little stale

3 large eggs, beaten

Chopped parsley, for serving

1 Preheat the oven to 350°F.

2 In a large skillet, heat the olive oil over medium heat. Add the mushrooms, onion, pepper flakes, and salt and pepper and cook, stirring occasionally, until the onion is mostly browned and frizzled, about 10 minutes, adding an extra drizzle of oil if necessary. Toss in the chard and cook until just wilted, about 3 minutes. Remove the pan from the heat.

3 Meanwhile, in a small saucepan, melt the butter over medium-low heat. Increase the heat slightly and stir in the mushroom powder. Whisk in the milk, then add the horseradish and heat until just warmed through. Remove the saucepan from the heat and let cool. Pour the milk mixture into a large measuring cup or medium bowl once it has cooled considerably.

PHOTOGRAPH ON PAGE 104

4   Grease a 9 × 13-inch baking dish with softened butter. Add half the bread cubes. Top with the mushroom/onion/chard mixture, spreading it into an even layer. Top with the remaining bread.

5   Once the milk mixture is cool, whisk in the eggs. Pour the milk-egg mixture over the bread, making sure every cube is a little damp. You can use your hands (or a spatula) to press down a little to compress.

6   Bake for 35 to 40 minutes. If it doesn't look toasty and golden enough, turn on the broiler to brown the top, 2 or 3 minutes. Remove from the oven and cool on a rack.

7   It's delicious served warm, but room temp is fine, too. Garnish with parsley.

NOTE: I call for mushroom powder here, a favorite secret weapon that I deploy to help along in the umami department. Once it's in your pantry, you'll use it for everything—soups, fried rices, and vegetable stir-fries, in particular.

Golden Greens Pie

SERVES 4 TO 6

There is a lot to love about this cousin of Greek spanakopita, known as hortopita (which translates to "greens pie"). For starters, it's the ideal way to use up those CSA greens that can sometimes have a habit of sticking around for too long, wilting in the fridge. I use kale and spinach here, but there's no reason why you shouldn't use one and not the other, or supplement with collards or chard or other sturdy greens. Another reason? I swap in regal, indulgent puff pastry for the usual phyllo dough. While you *do* have to remember to thaw the puff pastry ahead of time (and all that requires is stashing it in the fridge overnight), once it's ready to go, it's ready to go. (Please know that I realize this tweak compromises the authenticity of the dish!) Lastly, I almost forgot . . . it's so good!

¼ **cup extra-virgin olive oil**

2 **large leeks,** white and light-green parts only, thinly sliced (about 2 cups) and washed well

12 **to 14 ounces fresh greens** (such as curly kale, chard, or spinach; I like a combination of 8 ounces kale to 6 ounces spinach), stripped of tough stems and midribs, leaves chopped

Kosher salt and freshly ground black pepper to taste

1 **(14-ounce) package frozen puff pastry,** such as all-butter Dufour brand, completely thawed

2 **large eggs**

5 **ounces crumbled feta cheese**

2 **tablespoons fresh lemon juice**

4 **medium scallions,** white and light-green parts only, finely chopped

½ **cup chopped fresh dill**

½ **cup chopped fresh mint**

1 Preheat the oven to 425°F.

2 In a large pot or Dutch oven, heat the oil over medium heat. Add the leeks and cook, stirring occasionally, until softened, about 6 minutes. Add the greens, season with salt and pepper, and cook, stirring often, until everything is wilted, about 10 minutes. (If necessary, add them in shifts, waiting for the first batch to wilt and create room before adding the next.) Remove to a large bowl and set aside to cool.

3 Using a rolling pin, roll out the puff pastry crust on a lightly floured surface to fit a 9-inch round pie plate or a 9-inch square baking dish. It should be large enough to be able to drape over the sides of the dish or plate by 1 inch.

4 Once the greens have cooled, whisk 1 of the eggs in a small bowl and then mix it into the greens along with the feta, lemon juice, scallions, dill, and mint. Add the filling to the baking dish or pie plate and drape the puff pastry over the dish, allowing for an inch of overhang. Whisk the second egg and brush it all over the dough. Bake until the crust is shiny, golden, and puffy, about 15 minutes. Remove and let cool before slicing into wedges (or squares if you used a square baking dish) and serving.

Mixed Mushroom Shepherd's Pie

MAKE-AHEAD | FREEZE IT

SERVES 4

This meat-free take on the pub classic is hearty (and delicious) enough to quash even the most vegetarian-skeptical eater at your dinner table. Mushrooms stand in for the meatiness of the usual chicken-pork-veal mix, leeks lend it a sweet, oniony depth, and the pinchiest pinch of nutmeg gives it a hint of sweet British-pub warmth. And—music to your advance planning ears—you can make the filling ahead of time, like on a Sunday, then freeze it until you're ready to serve; thaw about an hour before you want to proceed with the recipe.

MASHED POTATO TOPPING

1¾ pounds Yukon Gold or baking potatoes, peeled and cut into large-ish chunks

Kosher salt, to taste

¾ cup whole milk, warmed

⅓ cup freshly grated Parmesan

2 tablespoons unsalted butter

¼ teaspoon ground white pepper

1 egg yolk (optional)

FILLING

4 tablespoons extra-virgin olive oil, plus more as needed

1¼ pounds (20 ounces) mixed mushrooms (I like shiitake and cremini), including trimmed stems (except the really woody ones), sliced

3 small or 2 medium leeks (8 to 10 ounces), finely chopped

3 small carrots (about 6 ounces), peeled and finely chopped

Kosher salt and freshly ground black pepper to taste

¼ teaspoon dried red pepper flakes

Pinch of freshly ground nutmeg (about ¼ teaspoon)

2 tablespoons tomato paste

1½ cups vegetable broth

2 tablespoons flour

½ cup whole milk

1 Make the mashed potato topping: Add the potatoes to a medium pot and cover with cold, salted water. Bring to a boil, then simmer for 15 to 20 minutes or until a knife cuts through a potato without any resistance. (Err on the side of overcooking since they are going to be mashed.) Strain and using a potato ricer, rice the potatoes into a large bowl (if you don't have a ricer, place them in a large mixing bowl). Add the milk, Parmesan, butter, white pepper, more salt, and the egg yolk (if using) and stir until smooth (or, if the potatoes are in the bowl, whip everything together with a hand mixer.) Set aside.

2 **Make the filling:** Heat the oven to 425°F. Add 3 tablespoons of olive oil to a large skillet set over medium heat. Add the mushrooms and cook until liquid releases and they shrink significantly, 10 to 12 minutes, stirring occasionally. Move them to one side of the pan, add the remaining tablespoon of olive oil to the empty side, then add the leeks, carrots, some salt and pepper, the red pepper flakes, and nutmeg. Cook for about 3 minutes, carefully stirring (avoid the mushrooms), until the leeks and carrots have softened, then mix everything together, adding a little more olive oil if you think the mixture looks dry.

3 Whisk the tomato paste with a tablespoon of water and stir into the vegetables, cooking until the tomato paste is fully integrated and looks a little darker and toastier in color. Stir in the vegetable broth, using a wooden spoon to scrape up any browned bits from the bottom of the pan. Whisk together the flour and milk in a measuring cup or small bowl and add to the vegetables. Turn up the heat to medium-high, and cook just until the broth is bubbly and slightly thickened. Remove from the heat.

4 Scrape the filling into a 9-inch pie dish, then spread the mashed potatoes on top. Bake for 15 minutes until the potatoes look golden on top, broiling for the last minute or two if you'd like. Serve warm, in heaping spoonfuls.

Sheet Pan Summer Pizza
WITH Corn & Tomatoes

UNDER 30 MINUTES

SERVES 4   This is the kind of dinner that shows up on the table on days when we don't have a plan. It's as good at room temperature as it is right out of the oven, especially for hot August days when you might want to make it ahead of time, to avoid blasting the oven late in the day. It's also delicious grilled—to do this, just generously brush the dough with olive oil, then grill on both sides, topping the dough with cheese and vegetables after the first flip, then covering.

3 tablespoons extra-virgin olive oil

1 (16-ounce) ball store-bought pizza dough, at room temperature

5 ounces mozzarella, pulled or sliced into stringy pieces (or shredded low-moisture mozzarella if grilling; see Note)

1½ to 2 cups cherry tomatoes (the sweetest you can find), halved

Kernels from 2 ears corn

¼ small red onion, sliced

Dash of garlic salt

Kosher salt and freshly ground black pepper to taste

Fresh thyme leaves or torn basil, for serving

1   Preheat the oven to 450°F.

2   Grease an 18 × 13-inch sheet pan with 2 tablespoons of the olive oil, then drop the ball of dough in the middle, pressing and stretching it out with your fingers so it reaches the edges. If it starts resisting the stretch, let the dough rest a few minutes and try again.

3   Scatter the mozzarella on top, leaving a 1-inch border around the edges. Sprinkle with the tomatoes, corn, and red onion. In a small bowl, mix the remaining 1 tablespoon olive oil with the garlic salt and brush this mixture around the perimeter of the pizza dough. Season all over with salt and pepper.

4   Bake until the cheese is bubbling and the crust looks golden-brown, about 15 minutes. Remove from the oven and top with thyme or basil before serving. The pizza is great hot, warm, or at room temp.

NOTE: If you're grilling, it's helpful to use low-moisture shredded mozzarella as opposed to the fresh mozz, which can get a little watery without the high blast of an oven's top heat.

Butternut Squash Galette
with Feta & Chiles

QUICK CLEANUP | UNDER 30 MINUTES

*SERVES 2 OR 3
(AS A MAIN)
OR 4
(AS A SIDE)*

There is one recipe like this in every cookbook I write—a dish that I've made so many times, is so easy, and so . . . everyday (in the best of ways), that I have to remind myself that other people will find novelty in it, and most likely add it to their rotation, too. The pickled chiles are a new addition for me, and, along with the salty feta, contrast with the sweetness of the roasted, concentrated squash in the most addictive way.

1 (9-inch) round pie dough, homemade or store-bought

1 small butternut or Honeynut squash (about 1 pound), peeled, halved lengthwise, seeded, and sliced into very thin half-moons

1 small yellow onion, halved and sliced into rings

2 tablespoons extra-virgin olive oil

1 tablespoon smoked paprika

Kosher salt and freshly ground black pepper to taste

4 ounces feta cheese, crumbled

¼ teaspoon garlic powder

1 large egg

½ cup chopped fresh parsley or dill

A dozen Jam-Jar Pickled Chiles (page 217), or to taste

1   Preheat the oven to 425°F. Line a sheet pan with parchment paper.

2   Place the pie dough on the lined sheet pan. In a bowl, toss together the squash, onion, olive oil, smoked paprika, and salt and pepper. Arrange the mixture in the center of the pie dough, laying the slices as flat as possible, and leaving a 1-inch border around the perimeter. Fold in the edges over the filling, overlapping as you work your way around the perimeter

as shown, and sprinkle the feta on the exposed vegetables. Season with more black pepper. In a small bowl, whisk the garlic powder with the egg, then brush the exposed dough with the egg wash.

3   Bake until the crust is golden and the cheese is melted, 20 to 25 minutes. Remove from the oven, top with the parsley and chiles, and serve in wedges, hot or at room temperature.

Green Curry Soup

QUICK CLEANUP | VEGAN

SERVES 4

Green curry is a simple, hearty soup from central Thailand, and it traditionally calls for green curry paste made from pounding chiles with various aromatics like makrut lime leaves, lemongrass, and cilantro. When I made this version, a decidedly nonauthentic one, my intent was to approximate the depth of that base flavor in half the time, so it might come together fast enough for weeknight cooking. The most obvious shortcut was picking up a jar of store-bought green curry paste, something I solved once I discovered the Mekhala brand, which is the perfect level of spiciness for me. (You could also use the more widely available Thai Kitchen brand.) As efficient as this recipe is, though, I feel it needs to be said that the meal also manages to be the perfect Sunday dinner—substantial and cozy, bright and stewy. And the beauty of the dish is that it is endlessly customizable; you can swap in rice for the noodles or broccoli for the bok choy.

1 (14- or 16-ounce) package extra-firm tofu, drained, cut into 1-inch cubes

Kosher salt

1 tablespoon neutral oil

1 small yellow onion, chopped

2 medium garlic cloves, minced

2-inch piece fresh ginger, peeled and minced

2 teaspoons minced fresh Thai red chiles (they can be super hot, so test before you chop and wear gloves when handling) or a shake of red pepper flakes (to taste)

Freshly ground black pepper to taste

3 tablespoons Thai green curry paste, such as Thai Kitchen or Mekhala

4 cups vegetable broth, preferably Better Than Bouillon (2 teaspoons mixed into 4 cups water)

1 Murasaki sweet potato (aka Japanese sweet potato) or a regular sweet potato, peeled and cut into ½-inch cubes

2 medium carrots, cut into ½-inch pieces

½ medium red bell pepper, cut into ½-inch pieces

10 to 12 pieces baby bok choy, halved lengthwise

6 ounces dried flat rice noodles

1 (15-ounce) can coconut milk (I use light, but full-fat works, too)

1 tablespoon tamari, or vegan fish sauce

Chopped fresh cilantro or Thai basil

Handful of bean sprouts (labeled ready-to-eat)

1 Season the tofu with salt, then transfer to a kitchen towel to drain for 10 to 15 minutes.

2 In a medium soup pot, heat the oil over medium heat. Add the onion, garlic, ginger, red chiles (or pepper flakes), and salt and black pepper and cook until the vegetables have slightly wilted, about 3 minutes. Smush in the green curry paste until it is integrated with the vegetables, then add the broth and bring to a low boil. Add the sweet potato, carrots, and bell pepper and simmer until they are cooked through, 8 to 10 minutes.

3 Add the bok choy and rice noodles and continue cooking until the bok choy is wilted and the noodles are cooked through (they should be tender, not chewy), about 5 minutes. Stir in the coconut milk, tamari, and tofu, and heat until warmed through.

4 Serve in bowls topped with cilantro and bean sprouts.

GREEN CURRY SOUP
(PAGE 120)

TRI-COLOR SLAW WITH
CRUNCHY CHICKPEAS &
YOGURT-CURRY DRESSING
(PAGE 141)

Dinner
Salads

&

Bowls

or

*How to eat more
Vegetables,
not just
eat less meat*

Recipes

THERE ARE REGULAR SALADS AND THEN THERE ARE dinner salads, which in my mind are different for a few reasons. For starters, protein is usually represented in some form—whether that's a nut, an egg, a bean or legume, or a cube of crispy tofu. Also? They just feel weightier, more dinner-worthy. They can hold their own as the only dish on the table—no soup on the side, or maybe not even a slice of bread to round it out. Lastly, most important, they are vegetable-focused, and therefore *beautiful*, and will remind you with each bite why you went down this plant-happy road in the first place.

Creamy Dill-Quinoa Salad
with Sweet Green Things & Tofu

MAKE-AHEAD

SERVES 4

Quinoa had its period of superstardom back in the aughts and my house couldn't get enough of it—until we did. Then I went through the complete opposite phase: No matter how I cooked the chenopod (not a grain, not a legume), it somehow always looked and felt like a big bowl of homework. Recently, two strategies have changed that for me: The first is playing around with the quinoa-to-stuff ratio, i.e., I started thinking about quinoa as another component of the salad, as opposed to a dominating base. For instance in this salad, it serves to both stretch out the green vegetables, and also allow them to shine a bit more than if they were buried under a mountain of quinoa. The second strategy is to add a little mayonnaise to the dressing. You only need a tablespoon to really lend the grains a more indulgent quality. I believe that's what they call a major glow-up.

CREAMY DRESSING

¼ cup white wine vinegar or champagne vinegar

1 teaspoon Dijon mustard

1 tablespoon regular or vegan mayonnaise

1 tablespoon honey

1½ teaspoons sambal oelek or sriracha sauce

Kosher salt and freshly ground black pepper to taste

½ cup extra-virgin olive oil

QUINOA BOWL

1 (14- or 16-ounce) package extra-firm tofu, drained, pressed, and cut into ½-inch cubes

3 tablespoons neutral oil, such as grapeseed (or olive oil in a pinch)

2 tablespoons soy sauce

1 tablespoon cornstarch

½ teaspoon cayenne pepper, or to taste (depending on desired heat level)

Kosher salt

1 cup quinoa (enough to yield 3 cups cooked)

8 ounces snow peas, ends trimmed, sliced

1 cup frozen shelled edamame, thawed

8 scallions, white and light-green parts only, finely chopped

½ cup finely chopped fresh dill

TO VEGANIZE: IN THE DRESSING, USE THE VEGAN MAYONNAISE OPTION AND REPLACE THE HONEY WITH 1 TABLESPOON AGAVE OR 1½ TEASPOONS SUGAR

1   Preheat the oven to 425°F. Line a sheet pan with parchment paper.

2   **Make the dressing:** In a small screw-top jar or measuring cup, combine the vinegar, mustard, mayonnaise, honey, sambal oelek, and salt and pepper. Shake or whisk the ingredients to combine. Add the olive oil and shake or whisk until the mixture is emulsified.

3   **Make the quinoa bowl:** In a medium bowl, toss the tofu with the neutral oil, soy sauce, cornstarch, and cayenne. Transfer the tofu to the prepared sheet pan and roast until browned and crispy around the edges, about 15 minutes. Remove from the oven and set aside to cool.

4   Meanwhile, in a saucepan, bring 1½ cups salted water to a boil. Add the quinoa, stir, cover, and reduce the heat to low. Cook until the water is completely absorbed and the quinoa is fluffy, about 20 minutes. Transfer the quinoa to a serving bowl to cool almost completely.

5   To the large bowl with the cooked quinoa, add the tofu, snow peas, edamame, scallions, dill, and creamy dressing. Toss gently to combine. Serve cold or at room temperature. (Chill in the fridge for a few hours or up to overnight; the flavors meld nicely.)

Grilled Halloumi Salad *with* Arugula & Peaches

QUICK CLEANUP | UNDER 30 MINUTES

So simple, yet so much happening in every bite here, between the peppery arugula, the sweet fruit, and the salty Halloumi. (Most brands of Halloumi are salty, which means you should be judicious with any extra seasoning.) If you don't have a grill basket for the nectarines, just halve them, brush with oil, and grill them on the grates, first cut-side down, then turning, until softened.

SERVES 2 OR 3 (AS A MAIN) OR 4 (AS A SIDE)

VINAIGRETTE AND GLAZE

1 teaspoon Dijon mustard

¼ cup balsamic vinegar

5 tablespoons extra-virgin olive oil

¼ small red onion, minced

Kosher salt and freshly ground black pepper
to taste

1 tablespoon pomegranate molasses

SALAD

12 ounces Halloumi cheese, halved horizontally and cut into about 3 × 1½-inch blocks

2 tablespoons neutral oil, such as canola or grapeseed

Kosher salt and freshly ground black pepper
to taste

3 nectarines or peaches, sliced

6 to 8 cups arugula (about 4 ounces)

¼ cup finely chopped fresh mint

Grilled bread (optional), for serving

1 In a small bowl, whisk together the mustard, vinegar, 4 tablespoons of the olive oil, the onion, and salt and pepper until combined. Set the vinaigrette aside. In another small bowl, whisk together the pomegranate molasses, the remaining 1 tablespoon olive oil, and salt and pepper. Set the pomegranate glaze aside.

2 Prepare a gas or charcoal grill to medium heat. Place the Halloumi on a plate, brush with 1 tablespoon of the neutral oil and season with pepper. Toss the nectarines with the remaining 1 tablespooon oil and arrange in a grill basket (see Headnote). Set on the grill

and cook, tossing, until they are slightly wilted and charred. Move to the cooler side of the grill so they are not over direct heat. (Or just remove the basket altogether.) Place the cheese blocks on the grill, turning each after a minute, then brushing with the glaze, continuing to turn until they attain grill marks and glisten, about 3 minutes.

3 While the fruit and cheese grills, toss the arugula with the vinaigrette in a large shallow bowl. Top the arugula with the nectarines and cheese. Garnish with the mint and serve.

Lentil Salad
WITH Jammy Tomatoes & Feta

MAKE-AHEAD

**SERVES 2 OR 3
(AS A MAIN)
OR 4
(AS A SIDE)**

This is the kind of recipe that is almost always on a big spread when I'm entertaining omnivores and vegetarians—it checks both the side-dish box and the main-dish box. And I'm forever grateful when there's some left over because the longer it sits in the refrigerator, the more tasty it gets.

BALSAMIC VINAIGRETTE

¼ cup extra-virgin olive oil

3 tablespoons white balsamic vinegar (see Note) or red wine vinegar

1 teaspoon Dijon mustard

Kosher salt and freshly ground pepper to taste

SALAD

1½ cups French, brown, or black beluga lentils

Kosher salt to taste

6 cups water or vegetable broth

14 to 16 jammy tomato halves (see page 218)

3 ounces feta cheese, broken into chunks

3 tablespoons chopped fresh dill

3 tablespoons chopped fresh chives

10 fresh mint leaves, minced

1 tablespoon minced red onion

Freshly ground black pepper to taste

1 Make the balsamic vinaigrette: In a small bowl, whisk together the olive oil, white balsamic vinegar, mustard, and salt and pepper until emulsified. Set aside.

2 Make the salad: In a medium pot, add the lentils to salted water and bring to a boil. Reduce to a simmer and cook until tender but still holding their shape, 15 to 20 minutes. Drain and let cool.

3 In a large shallow serving bowl, gently toss the lentils with the jammy tomatoes, feta, dill, chives, mint, red onion, and dressing. Season with salt and pepper. Serve warm, chilled, or at room temperature.

NOTE: I call for white balsamic vinegar here, but many can be cloyingly sweet. If you can't find a nice dry white balsamic, use red wine vinegar instead.

TO VEGANIZE: OMIT THE FETA

Farro Piccolo *WITH* Crispy Mushrooms & Parm

(WITH OR WITHOUT AN EGG)

MAKE-AHEAD | UNDER 30 MINUTES

SERVES 4

I thought about naming this "not your usual farro salad" because, is it just me? Or can farro be . . . a bit of a yawn sometimes? Not this recipe! The first time I made it, I was in a mild panic. Two of Abby's friends were coming over at the last minute for dinner, both of them soccer players with healthy appetites, and I was worried our dinner (soup and a salad!) wasn't going to cut it for them. The refrigerator was skeletal in the "fresh" department, with only two packs of mushrooms and a nearly wilted bunch of parsley. But when I spied an almost depleted bag of farro piccolo (also known as einkorn, an ancient grain that is smaller and nuttier that regular farro, and quicker to cook, too) in the pantry, the plan became very obvious, very fast. Between the mushrooms and the generous amount of Parm I added, the dish had, in Abby's words "almost too much umami." (Is there such a thing?) The lemon and parsley added brightness, and later, when it moved from side dish to the main event, the egg made it dinner.

1½ cups farro piccolo (see Note), enough to yield 6 cups of cooked farro

3 tablespoons extra-virgin olive oil, plus more as needed

2 (10-ounce) packages cremini mushrooms, thinly sliced

1 small yellow onion, roughly chopped

¼ teaspoon red pepper flakes

Kosher salt and freshly ground black pepper to taste

4 large eggs (optional)

1 cup freshly grated Parmesan cheese, plus more for serving

3 tablespoons fresh lemon juice

½ cup chopped fresh parsley

TO VEGANIZE: OMIT THE EGG AND REPLACE THE PARMESAN WITH ¼ CUP NUTRITIONAL YEAST

(continued on page 136)

1   Cook the farro according to the package directions. Drain and transfer to a medium serving bowl.

2   Meanwhile, in a large skillet, heat the olive oil over medium heat. Add the mushrooms (it's okay if the mushrooms are piled up on top of each other at first—as their liquid cooks off they will shrink and start getting crispy around the edges). Stir every few minutes, adding more oil as necessary, and after about 10 minutes, once they are browned (but not fully crisp), add the onion, pepper flakes, and salt and pepper. Cook, stirring often, until the onion is soft and sweet, about 5 minutes.

3   If serving with soft-cooked eggs, bring a medium pot of water to a boil. Using a slotted spoon, carefully lower the eggs into the water, turning the heat down slightly so the boil is controlled and not aggressive. Set your timer for 7 minutes, not a second more or less. While the eggs are simmering, prepare an ice bath by filling a bowl large enough to fit your eggs with ice and water. When your timer goes off, immediately transfer the eggs to the ice bath. Remove after a minute or two, peel gently, and slice in half.

4   Slide the mushroom-onion mixture into the farro, then toss in the Parm, lemon juice, and parsley.

5   Serve in bowls, each topped with a halved 7-minute egg (if using) and more Parm to taste.

NOTE: Yes, you can make this with regular farro, but I do encourage you to seek out the piccolo, which, because of its size, has zero hints of the mushiness its larger cousin can occasionally possess.

Kale Salad *with* Black Beans, Queso & Creamy Salsa Dressing

MAKE-AHEAD

SERVES 4

This dinner might be considered the vegetarian cousin of a traditional Tex-Mex taco salad and I've been making a version of it for years, finally landing on one that felt right after making three crucial swaps: beans for the ground beef, shredded kale for iceberg, and yogurt instead of sour cream in the dressing. It's quickly become a family favorite. It's certainly not imperative to use *blue* tortilla chips, but they really do make this salad look festive.

CREAMY SALSA DRESSING

⅓ cup extra-virgin olive oil

¼ cup plain yogurt or nondairy yogurt

¼ cup red wine vinegar

2 tablespoons salsa

Kosher salt and freshly ground black pepper to taste

SALAD

1 bunch Tuscan (lacinato) kale, stems and midribs removed, and shredded into confetti-like strands

Kernels from 3 ears sweet corn, uncooked

1 bunch scallions, minced

2 cups chopped sweet tomatoes (any kind: heirloom, cherry, etc.)

1½ cups cooked black beans, or 1 (15-ounce) can, drained and rinsed

4 ounces queso fresco or feta cheese, crumbled

1 avocado, cut into small cubes

1 cup blue corn tortilla chips, roughly crumbled (you don't want dust, you want pieces)

1 cup minced fresh cilantro

1 jalapeño, minced (including seeds and pith as desired for heat)

TO VEGANIZE: USE THE NONDAIRY YOGURT OPTION AND OMIT THE QUESO FRESCO

1 **Make the creamy salsa dressing:** In a small bowl or screw-top jar, combine the olive oil, yogurt, vinegar, salsa, and salt and pepper and whisk or shake until emulsified.

2 **Make the salad:** In a large salad bowl, combine the kale, corn, scallions, tomatoes, beans, cheese, avocado, corn chips, cilantro, and jalapeño. Toss with the dressing just before serving.

KALE SALAD WITH BLACK BEANS, QUESO
& CREAMY SALSA DRESSING
(PAGE 137)

Tri-Color Slaw *with* Crunchy Chickpeas & Yogurt-Curry Dressing

MAKE-AHEAD

SERVES 4

Are you wondering if I meant *crispy* chickpeas? The kind you fry or roast in the oven that are crisp on the outside and tender on the inside? I did not! A crunchy chickpea is a whole new ball game, and its main purpose, at least in the case of this salad, is to add texture. It should snap with crunch, like a fried Chinese noodle or, if I may be so bold, a Grape-Nut! It should be so crunchy that it is essentially hollow in the middle. How do you get your chickpeas this way? Well, you could make them yourself by roasting a 15-ounce can of garbanzos. Or you could just pick up a bag of store-bought snacking chickpeas, like the Saffron Road brand, which hit the mark every time. What you must *not* do, however, is toss the salad with the dressing until the moment before it is served. I know this will be hard for people out there like me, who want to have things organized and done ahead of schedule, but that will serve only to demote the crunch into *barely* a crisp.

DRESSING

½ cup plain yogurt (whole-milk or 2%)

2 tablespoons fresh lime juice (from about 1 small lime)

3 tablespoons extra-virgin olive oil

1 tablespoon, plus 1 teaspoon Madras curry powder (or curry powder plus ¼ teaspoon cayenne pepper, or more to taste)

1 teaspoon honey

Kosher salt and freshly ground black pepper to taste

SALAD

6 cups shredded cabbage (I like half red cabbage, half savoy)

2 cups shredded baby or large-leaf spinach (about 2 ounces)

1½ cups store-bought crunchy chickpeas (see Note), such as Saffron Road brand

½ cup store-bought fried onions or minced fresh scallions

½ cup golden raisins

⅓ cup finely chopped fresh mint

⅓ cup finely chopped fresh cilantro

Kosher salt and freshly ground black pepper to taste

(continued on next page)

1 **Make the dressing:** In a small food processor, combine the yogurt, lime juice, olive oil, curry powder, honey, salt and pepper, and 2 tablespoons of water and process to blend. Taste—maybe you like more lime? More heat? More salt? Adjust and set aside.

2 **Make the salad:** Just before you're ready to eat, in a large bowl, toss together the cabbage, spinach, crunchy chickpeas, fried onions, golden raisins, mint, and cilantro. DO NOT toss ahead of time—it's important that the onions and chickpeas (and cabbage for that matter) retain their crunch. Season with salt and pepper. Toss.

3 Drizzle the dressing over the salad, carefully tossing everything together until just mixed. Eat right away.

NOTE: If you can't find crunchy chickpeas, toss a 15-ounce can of chickpeas (drained and patted dry) with 2 tablespoons olive oil, salt, and a pinch of cayenne. Roast at 450°F for 25 minutes. Keep an eye on them, they should be dark brown, but not burnt.

TO VEGANIZE: IN THE DRESSING, REPLACE THE HONEY WITH AGAVE AND REPLACE THE PLAIN YOGURT WITH NONDAIRY YOGURT OR CASHEW CREAM

Crispy Honey-Harissa Glazed Chickpea Bowls *with* Yogurt & Mint

UNDER 30 MINUTES

SERVES 4

There are a couple things to know about this bowl before making it. The first is that it is GREAT. I always think I'm going to want rice or bread with it, but the yogurt and the chickpeas join forces to deliver a highly satisfying, legitimately filling meal. Next: You want the chickpeas to be crunchy-crispy, which means they should be almost dark brown when you take them out of the oven. To that end, make sure your chickpeas are as dry as possible before they go into the oven in the first place, whether you are using canned or from-scratch beans. Lastly, the heat level of harissa, a North African red pepper paste that should be in everyone's refrigerator, varies from brand to brand, so you'll want to taste the glaze and toss into the chickpeas accordingly.

3 cups cooked chickpeas, or 2 (15-ounce) cans, drained and rinsed, patted completely dry or air-dried for as long as possible

⅓ cup plus 4 tablespoons extra-virgin olive oil

Kosher salt and freshly ground black pepper to taste

3 tablespoons harissa paste

3 tablespoons honey

1 tablespoon light brown sugar

3 tablespoons unsalted butter, cut into small cubes

1 large head Bibb lettuce, torn into pieces (about 8 cups)

¼ cup fresh lemon juice (from about 1½ lemons)

Heaping ¼ cup plain Greek yogurt (any fat content, but I like at least 2%)

¼ small red onion, minced

½ cup chopped fresh mint

½ cup chopped fresh parsley

(continued on next page)

1   Preheat the oven to 450°F. Line a sheet pan with foil.

2   Spread the chickpeas on the lined pan and toss with ⅓ cup of the olive oil, salt and pepper. Roast until the chickpeas are crunchy-crispy, about 30 minutes, stirring every 5 to 10 minutes to prevent sticking. Meanwhile, line a medium bowl with paper towels and have near the oven.

3   While the chickpeas are roasting, in a small saucepan, combine the harissa, honey, brown sugar, and some salt and simmer over medium heat until the sugar has dissolved completely. Remove the pan from the heat and while the glaze is warm, stir in the butter.

4   When the chickpeas are done, make a "chute" out of the foil and pour the chickpeas into the towel-lined bowl, lightly blotting any excess oil. Let sit for a minute to drain, then slip the paper towel out of the bowl. Season the crispy chickpeas with salt and pepper.

5   Depending on how spicy your harissa is, and how spicy you like your food, start by adding 2 tablespoons of the glaze to the chickpeas, and gently tossing. (They should be glazy, not goopy.) Taste and add more glaze as desired.

6   Divide the lettuce among four bowls, season each with salt, pepper, about 1 tablespoon of fresh lemon juice, and 1 tablespoon olive oil, tossing to combine. Divide the glazed chickpeas among the bowls and top with dollops of yogurt, minced onion, mint, parsley, and more black pepper.

Crispy Eggplant Bowls
with Pistachios & Basil

UNDER 30 MINUTES

SERVES 4

Historically when I find myself eating dinner by myself, I almost always fall back on cheesy scrambled eggs or an easy, indulgent pasta like cacio e pepe, two meals that pair excellently with cold wine and bad TV. But recently, a new recipe—this recipe—entered that elite rotation. I live with people who feel neutral about eggplant. I, in fact, used to be that person, too, until I went down the plant-forward road and unlocked a real craveable love for the vegetable. Which means, when the haters are not home, I need to take full advantage. In this recipe, the eggplant slices really play the starring role, getting all crispy around the edges and melty in the middle. If I'm feeling motivated, I'll drizzle the final product with a tahini dressing, but just as often I take the easy way out and spoon some chili crisp on top. The recipe is written to serve four instead of one, because I believe your family, unlike mine, will actually get it. It is vegetarian comfort food at its best.

1½ cups white rice (enough to yield a little more than 4 cups cooked)

Juice of 1 small lime

Kosher salt to taste

1 Italian eggplant (about 1 pound), cut into ⅛-inch-thick rounds

3 tablespoons cornstarch

2 teaspoons za'atar

Freshly ground black pepper to taste

½ cup neutral oil, plus more as needed

3 fresh basil leaves, stacked, rolled, and sliced into ribbons

3 to 4 scallions, white and light-green parts only, finely sliced

⅓ cup salted roasted pistachios or cashews

Sweet and Spicy Tahini Dressing (page 206) or store-bought chili crisp

TO VEGANIZE: SKIP THE TAHINI DRESSING AND GO FOR THE CHILI CRISP.

1 Prepare the rice according to the package directions. Remove from the heat and stir in the lime juice and salt. Cover askew to keep warm.

2 Place the eggplant slices on a large cutting board or plate and sprinkle them generously with salt. Let sit for 10 minutes, then pat the pieces dry with paper towels. (This process helps draw out the moisture to create a more tender texture.)

3 Meanwhile, in a shallow bowl, stir together the cornstarch, za'atar, and salt and pepper. Add the eggplant slices to the bowl a few at a time, turning each slice until slightly coated.

4 In a large deep skillet, heat the oil over medium-high heat until the oil looks shiny. Working with a few slices at a time and wiping the pan every few rounds, add the eggplant and fry, flipping gently, until both sides are golden and crispy. Be patient, it could take up to 3 to 4 minutes per side. Remove with tongs or a slotted spoon and drain on paper towels.

5 Once all the eggplant is fried and crispy (add more oil as needed), divide the eggplant evenly among four bowls of rice and top with the basil, scallions, pistachios, and tahini dressing or chili crisp.

Summery Sicilian Eggplant Parm

MAKE-AHEAD

SERVES 4

In the spring of 2023, I hosted a food tour in Sicily, which sounds like I'm some kind of expert, but in fact, my job mostly consisted of hanging out with *Dinner: A Love Story* newsletter readers and traveling from town to town, vineyard to vineyard, dairy farm to dairy farm, exploring the rich agricultural tradition of the island. At every stop, there was an epic lunch, and at every epic lunch, there was a variation of this eggplant salad. Like the best Italian food (like the best food food), the eggplant was prepared simply: sliced very thin, cooked with a little garlic or salt and pepper, then served chilled or at room temperature along with a sharp or salty cheese like ricotta salata or Parm. Naturally, there was usually a plate of fresh tomato slices somewhere on the table, too, so I started combining them, eventually landing on a sort of deconstructed eggplant Parmesan, but a summer version, and one that is not nearly as cheesy or saucy as its wintry cousin. (Not that there's anything wrong with cheesy or saucy, but it's not necessarily the way I want my eggplant on a steamy August night.) Best of all, it was easy enough to replicate at home.

1½ pounds eggplant (either a few thinner Chinese eggplants or a large globe eggplant), cut into ¼-inch-thick rounds

Kosher salt to taste

1 pound tomatoes, any size or shape, the best and ripest you can find, chopped (about 2 cups)

5 chopped fresh medium basil leaves

1 small garlic clove, pressed

2 tablespoons extra-virgin olive oil, plus more for frying

Freshly ground black pepper to taste

1 (8-ounce) ball fresh mozzarella, sliced into pieces roughly the same size as your eggplant slices

Flaky sea salt

Freshly grated Parmesan cheese, for serving

Crusty bread (optional), for serving

TO VEGANIZE: OMIT THE CHEESES

(continued on next page)

1   Lay out the eggplant slices on a large cutting board and sprinkle a little kosher salt all over. This helps them sweat out the moisture to allow for a more concentrated flavor. Let sit about 10 minutes or as long as you have.

2   Meanwhile, in a small bowl, combine the tomatoes, basil, garlic, olive oil, and kosher salt and pepper. Toss and let sit, allowing the flavors to meld.

3   Using a paper towel, blot the liquid off the eggplant slices.

4   Pour ½ inch oil into a deep skillet and heat over medium-high heat until rippling and hot. Working in batches if necessary, add the eggplant slices and cook until slightly browned on both sides, about 5 minutes total, using tongs or a fork to turn them over midway through cooking. Remove to a paper towel to drain and set aside to cool.

5   Place the eggplant slices on a platter, alternating with the mozzarella slices. (The artfulness of this process is whatever time and inclination allows for.) When ready to serve, spoon the chopped tomato sauce all over the eggplant. Serve with sea salt, Parmesan, and crusty bread, if desired.

Dinner Fattoush

MAKE-AHEAD

SERVES 4

For years, I've made a version of cookbook author Leah Koenig's fattoush for Rosh Hashanah, the Jewish New Year. It's simple and bright, and a perfect side dish to compliment the usual center-of-the-table brisket or roast chicken. But I craved a version of the salad that was worthy of a stand-alone dinner, to be the showstopper itself, so I started bulking it up with pea shoots, sprouts, potatoes, and beans. It's a gorgeous, vibrant salad, the ultimate way to take advantage of peak-season tomatoes, and I encourage you to seek out the most colorful vegetables you can for optimal effect.

Dressing

½ cup plain whole-milk or low-fat yogurt

2 tablespoons extra-virgin olive oil

3 tablespoons fresh lemon juice

2 teaspoons za'atar

½ teaspoon garlic powder

½ teaspoon sugar

Kosher salt and freshly ground black pepper to taste

Salad

1 cup arugula sprouts, watercress, or pea shoots

1 cup tender greens (baby arugula or Bibb lettuce)

2 cups peak-season tomatoes, any kind, chopped or halved into 1-inch pieces

1½ cups cooked large white beans (such as lima, gigante, or butter) or garbanzo beans, or 1 (15-ounce) can, drained and rinsed

1 cup crumbled store-bought pita chips

3 medium potatoes or 12 to 15 small potatoes (purple for wow effect, but regular red potatoes will do), cooked and quartered or halved if small

3 mini English cucumbers (or 1 large), very thinly sliced

5 radishes, thinly sliced

3 tablespoons finely chopped red onion

¼ cup roughly chopped fresh flat-leaf parsley

⅔ cup crumbled feta cheese

TO VEGANIZE: IN THE DRESSING, REPLACE THE PLAIN YOGURT WITH NONDAIRY YOGURT. OMIT THE FETA FROM THE SALAD.

1 **Make the dressing:** In a small bowl, whisk together the yogurt, olive oil, lemon juice, 2 tablespoons water, the za'atar, garlic powder, sugar, and salt and pepper.

2 **Make the salad:** In a large bowl, toss together the arugula, greens, tomatoes, beans, pita chips, potatoes, cucumbers, radishes, red onion, parsley, and feta. Drizzle the dressing over the top and gently toss to combine. Serve immediately.

NOTE: If you are using canned beans, let them marinate in the dressing while you prepare the rest of the salad. I find this is an effective technique for freshening them up.

Smoky Black Bean Bowls
WITH Herby Eggs & Avocado

UNDER 30 MINUTES

SERVES 4

The suggested toppings here include avocado and sour cream, but if you don't have them, it's okay. The whole point of this meal is that all the ingredients should be pantry staples, and I'd be surprised if you didn't have everything you need to make it right now. Please note that it also makes an excellent breakfast.

SMOKY BLACK BEANS

3 tablespoons neutral oil, such as canola or vegetable (or extra-virgin olive oil in a pinch)

½ small yellow onion, finely chopped

1 cup chopped fresh tomatoes (any kind)

Kosher salt and freshly ground black pepper to taste

1 large garlic clove, minced

2 teaspoons tomato paste

1 tablespoon plus 1 teaspoon smoked paprika

¼ teaspoon ground cumin

Pinch of cayenne pepper (optional)

3 cups cooked black beans (½ cup cooking liquid reserved), or 2 (15-ounce) cans, drained and rinsed

FOR THE BOWLS

1 tablespoon unsalted butter (or oil, if you'd like it to be dairy-free)

4 large eggs

⅓ cup finely chopped fresh cilantro

Kosher salt and freshly ground black pepper to taste

Cooked rice (optional)

¼ small red onion, minced

1 avocado, chopped

1 Make the smoky black beans: In a medium pot, combine the oil, onion, tomatoes, and salt and black pepper and cook over medium heat, stirring, until the onion is soft, about 3 minutes. Add the garlic, tomato paste, smoked paprika, cumin, and cayenne (if using), stirring everything together and allowing the tomato paste to sizzle and toast for about a minute. Toss in the beans and reserved bean cooking liquid (or ½ cup water if using canned beans) and heat until everything has warmed through and the beans have soaked in the spices, 10 to 15 minutes. (The beans should be slightly stewy; if they aren't, add a little more water to loosen them up.)

2 Meanwhile, for the bowls: In a nonstick skillet, heat the butter (or oil) over medium-low heat. In a bowl, whisk together the eggs, cilantro, and salt and pepper and pour into the skillet. Let sit without stirring to allow the eggs to set. Flip once the eggs are mostly cooked around the edges. (You can also cut the omelet in half with your spatula if it's easier for you to flip that way.) Slide the eggs from the skillet onto a cutting board and slice into bite-size pieces.

3 Divide the beans and the eggs among four bowls (or over four bowls of rice, if using) and serve with the red onion and avocado.

TAGLIATELLE WITH CHICKPEAS
& ROSEMARY (PAGE 168)

Pasta

&

Noodles

or

when you need to feed the beasts

Recipes

WHEN OUR GIRLS WERE YOUNGER, WE ALWAYS BROUGHT them along to friends' houses for dinner and the reverse was true, too: We didn't even have to specify whether or not kids were invited to our house, it was just assumed. But then all our grade schoolers grew up and—shocker—opted to hang out with their friends instead of listening to a bunch of fogies discuss, say, the town's parking problems on a Saturday night. It's what is supposed to happen, everyone says, and I understand this, but it doesn't mean it doesn't bum me out, especially since teenagers bring such a distinct and fun energy to the table. So I am always thrilled when we can somehow convince our friends' teenagers to come over—a thrill quickly eclipsed by a specific, familiar terror. Maybe I'm just scarred by that time my then-sixteen-year-old nephew came over and ate an entire rack of ribs by himself without stopping to breathe, but when growing teenagers are in the equation, I'm always anxious that they won't be as excited by the tofu-cabbage salad as I am.

Enter: Pasta. It's universally loved and, along with pizza, one of the few family-friendly dinners where people don't necessarily assume that meat will be present. An aromatic, garlicky spaghetti, a cheesy baked lasagna, a chilled noodle salad on a hot summer night. Whether you're cooking for the neighborhood or just the one or two hungry beasts around your kitchen table, pasta is always the right call.

Warm Orzo Salad *with* Marinated Artichokes & Goat Cheese

QUICK CLEANUP | UNDER 30 MINUTES

SERVES 4

So many lightning-quick tricks in this family favorite—first, I love that the recipe relies on the same pot of water to cook both the beans and the orzo. Second, when you use an entire jar of marinated artichokes, the marinade combines with the melting goat cheese to create a creamy-tangy sauce for the orzo. And, congrats, you didn't do any work (or use any pots) to get it there. Before you add the marinade to the salad, taste a spoonful to make sure it has enough flavor. If it doesn't, tweak with a drizzle of olive oil, red wine vinegar, or oregano as needed, to taste. Also important: Usually, I like my green beans to have a little crunch, to be al dente, but this dish benefits from a more tender consistency. Lastly, if it's summertime, I'll often toss in a handful of fresh chopped tomatoes (heirloom or cherry or the sweetest you can find), which offers a nice contrast to all the tang.

Kosher salt

12 ounces green beans, ends trimmed, and cut into roughly 2-inch pieces

1½ cups orzo pasta

1 (12-ounce) jar Italian marinated artichokes

4 ounces goat cheese, cut into small pieces

½ cup finely chopped fresh basil

Freshly ground black pepper to taste

1 Bring a large pot of salted water to a boil. Prepare a large bowl of ice water. Add the green beans to the boiling water and cook until they are tender, about 5 minutes. Using a slotted spoon or a frying spider, scoop the beans into the ice bath to shock them, then drain in a sieve and place in a large serving bowl.

2 Return the hot water to a boil, add the orzo, and cook to al dente according to package directions (usually 6 to 8 minutes). Drain the orzo into the sieve you used for the beans.

3 Add the orzo, marinated artichokes, goat cheese, basil, and salt and pepper to the serving bowl holding the beans and toss everything until the goat cheese melts and combines with the marinade to coat the pasta like a sauce. Serve right away or refrigerate for up to 24 hours to allow the flavors to meld. Reheat over low heat on the stovetop and serve warm.

TO VEGANIZE: OMIT THE GOAT CHEESE AND ADD AN EXTRA DRIZZLE OF OLIVE OIL AND RED WINE VINEGAR.

Orecchiette *with* Tomato-Bean Summer Sauce

QUICK CLEANUP

SERVES 4

Here, beans upgrade a classic summer pasta sauce and bring two important things to the party: For starters, protein for the skeptics who often scratch their heads about that piece of the vegetarian puzzle. And second, consistency. Mashing up some of the beans, then distributing that starchiness with the tomato juices, helps thicken the sauce and give the pasta a delicately luxurious coat.

Kosher salt

1 pound short pasta (orecchiette is my top choice because they scoop up the tomatoes)

4 tablespoons extra-virgin olive oil

3 large garlic cloves, minced (or more, to taste; we aren't a huge garlic family)

½ small onion or 1 shallot, minced

½ teaspoon Calabrian chile powder or red pepper flakes

Freshly ground black pepper to taste

1½ cups cooked white beans, such as navy, butter, or cannellini, or 1 (15-ounce) can, drained and rinsed

6 cups diced fresh tomatoes (any kind, but preferably ripe and sweet; I like yellow and red cherry)

1 cup freshly grated Parmesan cheese

½ cup packed fresh basil leaves, shredded or torn

Ricotta or burrata (optional), for serving

TO VEGANIZE: OMIT THE CHEESES

1   Bring a large pot of salted water to a boil and cook the pasta to al dente according to the package directions. Drain and toss with 1 tablespoon of the olive oil while the pasta is in the colander to prevent sticking.

2   Place the pasta pot back on the stovetop over medium heat and add the remaining 3 tablespoons olive oil, the garlic, onion, chile powder, and salt and pepper and cook until aromatic and wilted, stirring occasionally, about 3 minutes.

3   Add the beans and season with salt and pepper. Using a fork or spatula, smash roughly half the beans into the pot, breaking them up to release their starch. (This will help thicken the sauce.) Stir in the tomatoes with their juices and bring to a boil. Decrease the heat to medium high and cook for 10 to 30 minutes to allow the tomatoes to break down—the longer the better, to allow for more concentration, but 10 minutes will do if that's all you've got!

4   Reduce the heat to low and add the pasta back to the pot with the tomatoes. Stir in the Parmesan and basil. Garnish with more black pepper and, if desired, dollops of ricotta or burrata.

Crispy Pan-Fried Gnocchi
WITH Peas & Chiles

QUICK CLEANUP | UNDER 30 MINUTES

SERVES 4

A few years ago, like the rest of the free world, my house went through a big Trader Joe's Cauliflower Gnocchi Phase, and even though a lot of people moved on, we did not. Especially since I discovered how delicious they are when pan-fried in olive oil until crispy, and also how easy it was to throw together for those nights when one of the girls had a late-night practice and needed dinner ten minutes ago. You can also use regular shelf-stable gnocchi if that's what's most convenient.

3 tablespoons extra-virgin olive oil, plus more for drizzling

1 pound Trader Joe's frozen cauliflower gnocchi, thawed as much as possible, or shelf-stable gnocchi

½ small yellow onion, chopped

Kosher salt and freshly ground black pepper to taste

1 cup frozen peas

1 teaspoon grated lemon zest

½ small serrano chile, sliced into thin rounds, seeded to desired heat preference

½ cup shredded pecorino cheese

Finely chopped fresh mint

1   In a large skillet, heat the olive oil over medium heat. When the oil is hot, add the gnocchi in one layer and cook without stirring until golden-brown (tip one over to check), about 5 minutes.

2   Add the onion and salt and pepper, tossing everything a bit so the gnocchi can brown a little on the other side. Cook until the onion is wilted, about 3 or 4 minutes. Add the peas and lemon zest and cook until the peas have warmed through.

3   Serve in bowls topped with the chile, pecorino, mint, and a drizzle of olive oil.

Pasta *WITH* Broccoli Pesto

QUICK CLEANUP | UNDER 30 MINUTES

SERVES 4

Here is one of those sneaky recipes that is actually many recipes in one. After discovering broccoli pesto, you'll never not see the potential for a vegetable to be pureed with olive oil and used as the starting point for indulgent, vegan sauces. Broccoli is the logical vegetable to teach you this technique because it's so vibrant and flavorful, but I've applied this same method to cauliflower, squash, and artichokes (see Shells with Artichoke Sauce, page 167!) with great success. Added bonus: I like that the entire recipe happens in one pot (plus one blender) and that the pasta boils in the same water as the broccoli. P.S. If you have more pine nuts, toasted extras for sprinkling on top would be excellent.

Kosher salt

5 cups roughly cut broccoli, including stalks (from 1 large head)

½ cup extra-virgin olive oil, plus more for drizzling

1 garlic clove, pressed

3 scallions, white and light-green parts only, roughly chopped

⅓ cup pine nuts

⅓ cup freshly grated Parmesan cheese, plus more for serving

2 tablespoons fresh lemon juice

Freshly ground black pepper to taste

1 pound pasta (I like spaghetti or fettuccine, but any pasta will work)

Red pepper flakes, for serving

TO VEGANIZE: OMIT THE PARM AND ADD 3 TABLESPOONS NUTRITIONAL YEAST WHEN YOU BLEND

1 Bring a large pot of salted water (at least 10 cups) to a boil. Add the broccoli and boil gently for 3 minutes. Using a slotted spoon, scoop out about one-third of the broccoli and set aside on a cutting board to cool, then chop finely. Continue to gently boil the remaining broccoli for another minute. Turn off the heat, scoop out ¼ cup of the broccoli water, then using a slotted spoon, scoop out the remaining broccoli and add it straight into a blender. (Excess water is ok.)

2 To the blender, add the olive oil, garlic, scallions, pine nuts, Parmesan, lemon juice, 1 or 2 tablespoons of the reserved broccoli water, and salt and pepper. Blend until emulsified and saucy (you want it to be easily pourable—thinner than a milkshake) using more broccoli water as needed.

3 Bring the pot of broccoli water back to a boil. Add the pasta and cook to al dente according to the package directions. If you've used up your reserved broccoli water, scoop out another ¼ cup of pasta water and set aside. Drain the pasta, drizzling in a little olive oil to prevent sticking. Return the pasta to the pot and toss in the pesto until it coats the pasta but doesn't look gloppy. (Use a drizzle of pasta water if needed.) Serve with red pepper flakes, the reserved chopped broccoli, and more Parmesan.

Shells *with* Artichoke Sauce & Crispy Capers

UNDER 30 MINUTES

SERVES 4

Amy Chaplin, one of the more influential plant-based heroes in my evolution, was the first person to show me the rich, silky sauce you can create by blending a humble 14-ounce can of artichoke hearts with scallions, olive oil, salt, pepper, and lemon juice. Much to my children's delight,* I've been directing way too much psychic energy toward thinking up other ways to use this technique, and eventually landed on this minimal-ingredient pasta dish. The mouthfeel is all rich and creamy, but there is no cream; the capers bring their briny pop, and the lemon gives it a nice bright and welcome quality for winter comfort food. P.S. This is vegan if you don't serve with the Parm.

*By delight, I mean "Really, *again*?"

Kosher salt

1 pound pasta shells

3 tablespoons extra-virgin olive oil, plus more for serving

1 medium shallot, sliced, or ½ small onion, chopped

1 large garlic clove, minced

Red pepper flakes to taste

Freshly ground black pepper to taste

1 cup Herby Artichoke Sauce (page 230)

Crispy Capers (page 223), about 1 tablespoon per serving

Freshly grated Parmesan cheese, for serving

TO VEGANIZE: OMIT THE PARM WHEN SERVING

1   Bring a large pot of salted water to a boil and cook the pasta to al dente according to the package directions. Reserving ½ cup of the pasta water (this is important!), drain the pasta and toss with 1 tablespoon of the olive oil in the strainer.

2   Return the pasta pot to the stovetop. Add the remaining olive oil, shallot, garlic, pepper flakes, and salt and black pepper and cook until the shallot is soft and golden, about 2 minutes. Reduce the heat to medium-low and slowly add the artichoke sauce to the pot, stirring

until everything is incorporated. Stir in a tablespoon or two of reserved pasta water at a time, until the sauce is warm and reaches the consistency of your favorite jarred pasta sauce. (I usually add about ¼ cup of pasta water.)

3   Reduce the heat to low and toss in the shells, stirring until everything is combined and well distributed. The pasta should have a nice shiny thin coating of sauce and not look thick and gloppy.

4   Serve in bowls topped with the crispy capers, Parmesan, and a drizzle of olive oil.

Tagliatelle *WITH* Chickpeas & Rosemary

UNDER 30 MINUTES

SERVES 4

Behold Exhibit A illustrating the concept of a recipe being more than the sum of its parts. The ingredients here are so everyday, and yet, when that garlic mixes with the white wine and is then spiked with the piney rosemary, something magical happens. As my friend and food stylist Lauren Radel said to me when she sat down to this dish, "Garlic and rosemary together is a gift to the world." I'd add wine to that, too. Missy Robbins, the James Beard Award–winning Brooklyn chef, makes a similar dish using pappardelle, which is a nice way to add a little drama, elevating it to Saturday night fare.

Kosher salt

1 pound egg tagliatelle, preferably the kind that comes in nests

¼ cup extra-virgin olive oil, plus more for drizzling

3 cups cooked chickpeas, or 2 (15-ounce) cans, drained and rinsed, patted dry as much as possible

Freshly ground black pepper to taste

⅔ cup dry white wine

3 garlic cloves, minced

2 tablespoons unsalted butter

1 cup freshly grated Parmesan cheese, plus more for serving

Needles from 1 fresh rosemary sprig, chopped, about 1 heaping tablespoon

1   Bring a large pot of salted water to a boil and cook the pasta to al dente according to the package directions. Reserving ¼ cup of the pasta water, drain the noodles and drizzle a little oil over them in the colander to prevent sticking.

2   Return the pasta pot to the stovetop, over medium heat. Add the ¼ cup oil, the chickpeas, and salt and pepper and cook until the chickpeas are crisp-tender, about 8 minutes. Using a slotted spoon, remove the chickpeas to a plate.

3   Add the white wine, scraping the bottom of the pan to release any crispy bits, then add the garlic and butter and cook until the garlic is golden and aromatic, about 1 minute.

4   Return the tagliatelle to the pot along with the Parmesan and rosemary and toss together, adding a drizzle of pasta water at a time if necessary to evenly distribute the cheese on the pasta. Toss in the reserved chickpeas, then serve with lots of black pepper and Parmesan.

Chilled Cabbage-Loaded Noodles

MAKE-AHEAD | VEGAN

SERVES 4

I've been making a version of this cold rice noodle salad ever since trying one in Hannah Che's cookbook, *The Vegan Chinese Kitchen*, and it has become a go-to dish on two occasions. The first is on a hot summer night. Not only is it cool and refreshing, but it's the kind of recipe that is easy enough to pull together in the morning, and then you get that tremendous feeling of satisfaction knowing that its flavors are intensifying while you go about the rest of the day. (But do make sure you toss it a few times throughout the day to prevent the noodles from sticking.) The other time I find myself making it is for guests. See above, re: make-ahead, but also, if you opt for vegan mayonnaise and use tamari instead of soy sauce: It's gluten-free, dairy-free, vegan, and has a commanding enough presence on the table to be the main dish. In other words, if this is on the spread, you've got all your guests, and all their various diets, covered.

NOODLES

8 ounces flat rice noodles

1 tablespoon toasted sesame oil

12 ounces napa cabbage (about 1 small head), shredded

1 large carrot, shaved into ribbons with vegetable peeler

2 small cucumbers, shaved into ribbons with vegetable peeler

5 scallions, white and light-green parts only, minced

1 cup frozen shelled edamame, thawed

2 tablespoons minced pickled ginger, or a 1-inch piece of fresh ginger, finely minced

DRESSING

¼ cup grapeseed oil

¼ cup tamari or soy sauce

1 tablespoon vegan mayonnaise or regular mayonnaise

1 tablespoon unseasoned rice vinegar

1 garlic clove, pressed or minced

½ teaspoon sriracha or hot sauce

FOR SERVING

¾ cup minced fresh cilantro

Chili crisp and/ or chopped salted roasted peanuts, for topping

1 **Make the noodles:** Cook the rice noodles according to the package directions, usually about 5 minutes. Drain and rinse under very cold water, which will wash off the excess starch and prevent the noodles from getting sticky and gummy. Transfer the noodles to a large bowl and immediately toss with the sesame oil.

2 Toss in the napa cabbage, carrot, cucumbers, scallions, edamame, and pickled ginger with the noodles.

3 **Make the dressing:** In a small bowl, whisk together the grapeseed oil, tamari, mayonnaise, rice vinegar, garlic, and sriracha.

4 Thoroughly toss the noodle-vegetable mixture with the dressing and refrigerate for at least 2 hours, tossing once or twice as it chills to prevent sticking.

5 **When ready to serve:** Finish with the cilantro and desired toppings.

White Lasagna
with Mint-Pea Pesto

MAKE-AHEAD

SERVES 4

One of the first recipes I ever wrote about on my blog, *Dinner: A Love Story*, was my friend Todd's mint-pea dip, which involved blending sweet peas with Parmesan, mint, and lemon juice to yield the greenest, spring-iest pesto, which we would then spread on bread or even use as a dip for potato chips. I equate the addictive dip with spring, even though I never use fresh peas—long ago I discovered that the flash-frozen peas in the freezer section are way more reliably sweet than most of the ones you find at farmers' markets (plus . . . they're shelled!). Over the years, I've found myself planning meals around Todd's minty peas, whether I'm serving the spread on thick slices of crusty toast and topping it with burrata, or layering it into a bright herby lasagna, as I do here. Unlike a lot of lasagna recipes meant to feed the masses, this recipe is made in an 8-inch square baking dish, the perfect size for a family of four on a regular old Tuesday night. (You could of course double it in a 9 × 13-inch dish for a larger group.)

1 (12-ounce) bag frozen peas, thawed

1 cup loosely packed fresh mint leaves

1 cup freshly grated Parmesan cheese

1 garlic clove, roughly chopped

Grated zest and juice of 1 medium lemon

½ cup extra-virgin olive oil

Kosher salt and freshly ground black pepper to taste

1½ cups whole-milk ricotta cheese (about one 15-ounce container)

1 large egg

Pinch of red pepper flakes

9 no-cook lasagna noodles

3 ounces mozzarella cheese, preferably low-moisture, sliced or shredded

1 Preheat the oven to 425°F.

2 In a food processor, pulse the peas, mint, ½ cup of the Parmesan, the garlic, lemon juice, ¼ cup water, the olive oil, and salt and pepper until it becomes a smooth puree. In a medium bowl, whisk together the ricotta, ¼ cup of the Parmesan, the lemon zest, egg, ⅓ cup water, the pepper flakes, and salt and pepper.

3 In an 8-inch-square baking dish, spread ¼ cup of the ricotta mixture over the bottom. Top with 3 lasagna noodles, overlapping them a little. Spread half of the mint-pea pesto over the noodles, then half of the remaining ricotta mixture. Arrange another 3 lasagna noodles on top, laying them perpendicular to the first layer of noodles. Set aside about 2 tablespoons each of both the pesto and the ricotta mixture, then cover the noodles with all of the remaining pesto and ricotta. Top with the remaining 3 lasagna noodles (lay them in the other direction) and spread the reserved pesto and ricotta on top. Sprinkle the top with the mozzarella and the remaining ¼ cup Parmesan.

4   Cover the baking dish with foil and bake until the noodles are tender, about 35 minutes. Remove the foil, set the oven to broil, and broil the lasagna until the cheese is browned and bubbling, 5 to 10 minutes.

5   Remove from the oven and rest 5 minutes before serving to allow it to set. (This makes it easier to cut.)

Brown Butter Orzo *with* Zucchini & Basil

QUICK CLEANUP | UNDER 30 MINUTES

SERVES 4

I like vegetable-packed pasta dishes like this where the noodle is not the dominating base, interrupted every now and then by a goodie. Here you taste the goodies—the brown butter and the caramelized zucchini in every bite. I often serve this dish when friends come over in the summer alongside a simple sliced tomato salad.

Kosher salt

1 pound orzo pasta

3 tablespoons extra-virgin olive oil

1 large garlic clove, halved

20 to 24 ounces zucchini (about 4 small), grated and squeezed dry in a kitchen towel (see Note)

¼ teaspoon red pepper flakes, or to taste

Freshly ground black pepper to taste

4 tablespoons unsalted butter

Shredded fresh basil, for serving

1 Bring a medium pot of salted water to a boil and cook the orzo to al dente according to the package directions.

2 While the orzo cooks, in a large skillet, heat the olive oil over medium heat. Add the garlic and cook until the garlic is golden and the oil is infused with its flavor, about 1 minute. Remove and discard the garlic, then add the zucchini, pepper flakes, and salt and black pepper and cook until the shreds have cooked down and turned golden and caramelized, 10 to 12 minutes. (Dark brown bits are not only okay, but desirable.) Turn off the heat and let sit in the pan.

3 When the orzo is done, drain and toss the pasta with 1 tablespoon of the butter right in the colander to prevent sticking.

4 Return the pasta pot to the stovetop, add the remaining 3 tablespoons butter, and set over medium-low heat. Do not leave your stovetop perch! (It can go from brown butter to burned butter in an instant.) Watch as the butter melts, then foams furiously, then begins to turn light brown, swirling occasionally as you go. The whole process should take about 4 minutes, but it's really an eyeball (and an aromatic) thing: As soon as it starts to smell nutty and you start to see the speckles at the bottom of the pan, remove the pan from the heat so the butter doesn't burn.

5 Toss the orzo and the zucchini with the brown butter. Serve in bowls with lots of fresh basil.

NOTE: It is crucial to squeeze the zucchini dry in a kitchen towel, which prevents the zucchini from getting mushy. See photo on page 93 for the technique.

SWEET POTATO / TAHINI TOASTS
WITH PECANS & SPROUTS
(PAGE 181)

Stuffed, Wrapped

&

Topped

OR

How to stock your freezer, fridge, and pantry to speed up dinner

Recipes

I HAVE VERY STRONG OPINIONS FOR AND AGAINST the shortcut products that abound in the supermarket, from the precubed butternut squash (love love love) to the prepeeled garlic in the plastic containers (what do you think I am, some kind of monster?). Weirdly, I would never deign to buy a bottle of additive-laden salad dressing, but have no problem picking up a jar of marinated peppers or artichokes and using the jar's marinade to help me along with a quick salad. Why? I don't know! Everyone has their own line in the sand in terms of what kitchen tasks they feel okay about conceding to the 30-minute dinnertime industrial complex. But I do find that there are a few nonnegotiables in this equation, and all of them play a role in the recipes in the following pages. They are all some form of starchy vehicle, i.e., components that inspire meals and help get you halfway to dinner: tortillas, empanada shells, pizza doughs, pie doughs, precooked grains, a good crusty bread that can sit in the freezer and be deployed when sandwich night calls. The recipes on the following pages are a salute to those ingredients, my loyal, dependable shortcut soldiers: See Store-Bought Saviors: The Complete List (page 26).

Sweet Potato/Tahini Toasts
with Pecans & Sprouts

MAKE-AHEAD | QUICK CLEANUP | VEGAN

MAKES 1½ CUPS (ENOUGH FOR 4 LARGE TOASTS)

There used to be a restaurant called Josie's on the Upper West Side of Manhattan that my friends and I patronized often in the 1990s. The prices were reasonable and you could almost always get a reservation for a large group. But the big draw, at least for me, was that they served a free curried sweet potato dip along with the free bread basket. It was so good that we often joked we didn't even need to order the rest of the dinner. A warm piece of bread with the spiced spread was a meal in itself. And even though Josie's closed in 2015, the spirit of the spread lives on in this toast. I make this often for company when the rest of the menu is rich and meaty, and also on a weeknight, when dinner calls for something easy, vegetarian, and still substantial.

1½ pounds sweet potatoes (about 2 medium)

3 tablespoons warm water

2 tablespoons plus 1 teaspoon tahini

1 tablespoon fresh lemon juice

1 teaspoon Madras curry powder (or regular curry powder plus ¼ teaspoon cayenne added to it)

¼ teaspoon ground cumin

Kosher salt and freshly ground black pepper to taste

4 slices bread (any kind: seeded, white, pumpernickel), cut about ½ inch thick, or to desired thickness

2 tablespoons olive oil

⅓ cup crushed toasted pecans

Baby arugula, pea shoots, or sprouts, for serving

1 Preheat the oven to 425°F.

2 Prick the sweet potatoes all over with a fork, place on a foil-lined sheet pan, and bake until their skin feels loose and shriveled, about 1 hour. Remove from the oven and set aside to cool.

3 Scoop the flesh from the sweet potatoes into a food processor. Add the warm water, tahini, lemon juice, curry powder, cumin, and salt and pepper and blend, adding extra water a tablespoon at a time, until the puree reaches a spreadable consistency, about the thickness of guacamole.

4 Toast the bread slices and drizzle them lightly with the olive oil. Spread the sweet potato mixture on top of each piece of toast, then top with the pecans and greens, and a few grinds of black pepper.

Tamarind-Glazed Cauliflower Tacos

UNDER 30 MINUTES

SERVES 4

My daughter came home from a sweet-16 party a few years ago and claimed she had just eaten hands-down the most amazing cauliflower tacos. "You sure they were cauliflower?" I asked her. "Yes," she said. "You don't like cauliflower, though," I reminded her. After a few follow-up questions, I determined that they had been deep-fried to resemble popcorn shrimp, something I wasn't interested in or capable of doing. But every few weeks, she'd say "Remember those cauliflower tacos?" not so much reminding me as daring me to replicate them at our own dinner table. It wasn't until I made a batch of New York chef Einat Admony's crispy cauliflower (one of her signature recipes where the fried cauliflower gets tossed with currants and pine nuts) that I realized I could achieve the same crispiness without completely deep-frying the florets. So that's what I did.

Kosher salt

1 large head cauliflower, cut into bite-size florets

⅔ cup all-purpose flour

1 teaspoon garlic powder

1 teaspoon freshly ground black pepper

Canola oil, for shallow-frying

8 hard taco shells

2 to 3 tablespoons store-bought tamarind sauce (such as Swad brand) or other glazy sauce (see Note)

FOR SERVING

Plain yogurt (whole-milk or nondairy)

Spicy Avo Sauce (page 227) or store-bought coriander chutney

TO VEGANIZE: TAKE THE NONDAIRY YOGURT OPTION FOR SERVING

1   Set up a large bowl of ice and water. Bring a large pot of salted water to boil. Add the cauliflower and boil until tender, about 2 minutes. Remove with a slotted spoon and drop into the ice bath to stop the cooking. Remove from the bath and place on paper towels to drain.

2   In a large resealable bag, combine the flour, garlic powder, salt, and the pepper. Add the florets, seal, and shake until thoroughly coated.

3   Pour ¼ inch of canola oil into a Dutch oven or large skillet and heat over medium-high heat until the oil is shiny. Line a serving bowl with paper towels and set near the stove.

4   Working in batches of about 1 cup of cauliflower at a time, carefully drop the florets into the oil and fry until they're golden-brown, turning occasionally, 3 to 5 minutes. Using a slotted spoon, transfer to the towel-lined bowl.

5   Meanwhile, wrap the taco shells in foil and warm them in a 350°F oven for 10 minutes. Remove and keep them wrapped in their foil.

6   Slip the paper towel out from under the cauliflower. Add the tamarind sauce to the cauliflower (start with 2 tablespoons, adding more if you like) and toss until the cauliflower is glistening and evenly coated.

7   **To serve:** Stuff the taco shells with the cauliflower and dollop with yogurt and avo sauce or chutney.

NOTE: The first night I attempted this recipe, I happened to have a homemade American barbecue sauce on hand, but for subsequent versions I used whatever glazy bottled sauce I had in the refrigerator door: store-bought barbecue, hoisin, and my favorite, tamarind.

TAMARIND-GLAZED
CAULIFLOWER TACOS
(PAGE 182)

Baked Pinto Bean Empanadas

FREEZE IT

I first attempted empanadas when food writer Bianca Cruz (my colleague who worked with me on volume one of *The Weekday Vegetarians*) shared her mother's empanada recipe with me for an article I was writing. I had the privilege of testing the recipe to make sure it worked. (I know, I know, how lucky am I?) Not only did it work, but I went nuts over the empanadas, and they sent me down a long path of empanada discovery. How had I never noticed the frozen empanada discs in the supermarket freezer section? How had I never used sazón seasoning, a staple of Puerto Rican cuisine that adds the kind of umami that makes people ask "What did you put in these?" (I played around with different combinations of beans and cheese, but always included that sazón.) The hardest thing about the recipe is remembering to thaw the discs (either by leaving them in the fridge overnight or letting them sit at room temperature for 15 to 20 minutes before baking), but otherwise, I routinely bake up a batch to stash in the freezer, then heat them for dinner eaters who need to eat earlier or later than the rest of us for whatever reason. According to Bianca, they're great with rice or freshly made maduros (fried ripe plantains).

1 tablespoon neutral oil, such as canola or vegetable (olive oil is fine in a pinch)

1½ cups cooked pinto beans (⅓ cup cooking liquid reserved), or 1 (15-ounce) can, drained and rinsed

1 small jalapeño, seeded if desired, and minced

2 tablespoons tomato paste

1½ teaspoons sazón (I like the Badia brand)

¼ teaspoon cayenne pepper

10 frozen 6-inch empanada discs, thawed

1½ cups shredded sharp cheddar cheese

1 large egg, beaten

Store-bought salsa

(continued on next page)

1   Preheat the oven to 400°F. Line a sheet pan with parchment paper.

2   In a medium skillet, heat the oil over medium heat. Add the beans, reserved bean cooking liquid (or ⅓ cup water if using canned beans), and the jalapeño and cook for 2 to 3 minutes while gently mashing the beans with the back of a silicone spatula or fork. (Add some water, 1 tablespoon at a time if it looks dry.) Add the tomato paste, sazón, and cayenne and mix well until the beans resemble refried beans. Remove from the heat.

3   Place the empanada rounds on the lined sheet pan. Spoon about 1½ tablespoons of the bean filling on one side of the round of dough and top with 1 to 2 tablespoons cheddar. Fold the dough over, creating a half-moon shape, and press lightly so it's flattish. Seal the empanada's seam together by pressing the edges with a fork. Repeat until you've worked through all of the empanadas.

4   Lightly brush each empanada with the beaten egg and use a sharp knife to poke a few holes in the top of each one to allow steam to escape.

5   Bake until the empanadas are golden-brown, 20 to 25 minutes. Cool briefly and eat warm or at room temperature with salsa. I almost always freeze some in a freezer bag, then reheat them individually wrapped in foil at 350°F for 20 minutes.

Sheet Pan Pizza *with* Asparagus, Boursin & Spring Onions

MAKE-AHEAD | QUICK CLEANUP

SERVES 4

I once excerpted a spring pizza recipe on my website and titled it "Pizza for Serious Pizza Lovers." It was from *Pizza Camp*, a cookbook by Joe Beddia, who is a Philadelphia-based pizza genius; not surprisingly, he went deep on technique and gear and pizza philosophy in general: His dough fermented for at least 24 hours before being ready; there was a "subrecipe" (a recipe within a recipe) for something called "spring cream" that called for a blender and a dozen or so ingredients (many of them herbs); and of course everything got baked on pizza stones and you needed a peel to get the pizza in—and out—of the oven. Obviously, the recipe was A-plus-plus-plus, the kind of pizza I wanted to make again as soon as I finished my last bite. But it was just . . . so much work. One night, when I had the craving, but not the energy, I shortcut the whole shebang, using store-bought pizza dough instead of homemade, herby Boursin cheese instead of the spring cream, and baked the whole thing on a boring old sheet pan, bypassing the peel and the stone completely. And you know what? No one will call me Joe Beddia, but in its own way, for a certain kind of cook, the recipe might be called genius.

16 ounces pizza dough (store-bought is fine)

1 bunch spring onions, or 1 large shallot or 2 bunches scallions, very thinly sliced

¼ cup red wine vinegar

4 tablespoons extra-virgin olive oil

6 ounces asparagus, woody ends trimmed

Kosher salt and freshly ground black pepper to taste

1 (5.2-ounce) container Boursin cheese

(continued on next page)

1 Preheat the oven to 450°F.

2 Remove the pizza dough from the refrigerator and leave at room temperature for at least 30 minutes and up to 3 hours. (This makes it easier to work with.) In a small jar, combine the spring onions (or shallots or scallions) and vinegar. Set aside.

3 As the oven heats, brush an 18 × 13-inch sheet pan with 1 tablespoon of the olive oil. (Or use your fingers.) Drop the dough in the center of the pan and, using your oiled fingers, press and stretch out the dough to the sides and into the corners of the pan. The goal is to get the crust as thin as possible. (If it resists, set it aside for another 10 minutes and then try again.)

4 In a small bowl, toss the asparagus with 2 tablespoons of the olive oil. Season with salt and a generous amount of pepper.

5 Using your fingers, drop small dollops of the Boursin cheese on top of the dough, leaving a 1-inch cheese-free border. Using a knife, gently spread and flatten the cheese until as much of the dough is covered as possible. Arrange the asparagus on top of the cheese—you can be as artless as you like here, no one is grading you, but I like lining them up irregularly so that every slice has at least a few bites of asparagus tips, my favorite part. Brush the perimeter of the dough with the remaining 1 tablespoon olive oil. Grind some more black pepper on top.

6 Bake until the crust looks golden and the asparagus looks crisp, about 15 minutes.

7 Serve warm or at room temperature, topped with the pickled onions.

Roasted Vegetable Reubens

UNDER 30 MINUTES

MAKES 4 SANDWICHES

Is it heresy to call something a Reuben if there is no corned beef anywhere to be found? Maybe, but I'm not sure I care—my daughter Abby first made one of these for me (yes, another one of her creations, this one inspired by a TikTok video) and they are about as good as what they're riffing on. They're equally satisfying if you stick to one vegetable—all Brussels sprouts or all broccoli. Just make sure whichever you are using, that it gets cooked to deep brown roastiness. When served with the cool, creamy dressing, the combo is addictive.

4 cups broccoli florets

4 cups trimmed and quartered Brussels sprouts (roughly the same size as the broccoli florets)

¼ cup extra-virgin olive oil

Kosher salt and freshly ground black pepper to taste

8 ounces Gruyère cheese, thinly sliced or grated

Russian Dressing (recipe follows)

8 slices rye bread, lightly toasted

About ½ cup prepared sauerkraut, for serving

1 Preheat the oven to 425°F. Line a sheet pan with foil or parchment paper.

2 Spread the broccoli and Brussels sprouts on the lined sheet pan and, using your hands, toss with the olive oil, and salt and pepper. Roast until very well cooked and crispy, about 20 minutes. (A few burned Brussels leaves are fine.)

3 Remove the sheet pan from the oven and gather the vegetables in 4 mounds, each about the size of the bread you will be serving them on. Set the oven to broil.

4 Top each pile of vegetables with one-quarter of the Gruyère and broil until the cheese is melted and bubbling, about 1 minute. Remove from the oven.

5 Spread as much dressing as you'd like on four of the toast slices. Using a spatula, lift up the mound of cheesy vegetables and place on top of the dressed toast. Top with sauerkraut and the remaining slice of toast. Halve and serve.

Russian Dressing

MAKES ⅔ CUP

½ cup mayonnaise

2 tablespoons fresh lemon juice

2 tablespoons chopped bread-and-butter pickles

2 tablespoons ketchup

1 tablespoon finely chopped white onion

¼ teaspoon smoked paprika

Kosher salt and freshly ground black pepper

In a small bowl, whisk together the mayonnaise, lemon juice, chopped pickles, ketchup, onion, smoked paprika, and salt and pepper to taste. Refrigerate until needed. (It will keep for 7 to 10 days.)

Miso-Mushroom Tacos
WITH Pickled Cabbage

UNDER 30 MINUTES | VEGAN

SERVES 4

This recipe began as a "serves one person" kind of thing. I had half a container of mushrooms, one onion, and one kid who had to eat before a late soccer practice. Looking for something fast that would fill her up but not weigh her down, I threw the mushrooms into a hot skillet and cooked them until they got crispy, and then scanned my fridge to figure out what might add something unexpected. Let me just say that the solution to this quandary in my house is almost always miso paste. Just a spoonful, thinned out with hot water, was all I needed to add that sweet-and-salty hit and win over my unsuspecting athlete . . . and eventually the whole family. Definitely opt for red cabbage when pickling—you'll want its texture here. Serve these tacos with white rice that's been tossed with lime juice and chopped cilantro.

1 teaspoon toasted sesame oil

3 tablespoons neutral oil or olive oil, plus more as needed

20 ounces mushrooms, any kind, stems trimmed, sliced

1 small yellow onion, finely chopped

3 tablespoons sweet white miso

1 teaspoon sriracha

2 tablespoons hot water

8 (5-inch) corn tortillas or hard taco shells

6 medium scallions, white and light-green parts only, minced

Rice Vinegar–Pickled Cabbage (page 220), for serving

1   In a large skillet, heat the sesame and neutral oil over medium heat. Add half the mushrooms and cook until they have mostly released all their liquid, then add the second half, mixing them in. Cook for 8 to 10 minutes total. Add the onion, and a drizzle of oil (if needed), and cook until softened, 4 to 5 minutes.

2   Meanwhile, in a small bowl or measuring cup, whisk together the miso, sriracha, and hot water until the mixture is the consistency of ketchup.

3   Stir the miso mixture into the mushrooms, then remove the

mushrooms from the heat.

4   Heat oven to 350°F. If you are using hard taco shells, place them on a sheet pan and place in the oven for 5 minutes. If using corn tortillas, place each one on a gas burner for 10 seconds per side, until the tortilla is slightly charred. (Or warm each in a nonstick or cast-iron pan set over medium-high heat.) Remove and keep warm under a foil tent.

5   When ready to serve, stuff each taco shell or tortilla with about ⅓ cup of the mushroom filling, then top with the scallions and pickled cabbage.

Crunchy Stuffed Red Peppers

QUICK CLEANUP

SERVES 4

I've always loved stuffed peppers as a vehicle for leftovers—whether it's stretching out last Sunday's shredded chicken or some leftover roasted vegetables in the fridge. But I also love them grain-stuffed, and once I discovered Trader Joe's 10-minute farro, they became an easy fallback option for a quick, healthy weeknight dinner. Important: These are not cereal bowls filled with endless scoops of filling. You want most bites to have a little of the crunch of the bread crumbs, so slice the peppers lengthwise and don't stuff them too deep. The eggs are optional, but they add an easy protein hit if you're looking for one.

3 cups cooked farro (or one bag of Trader Joe's 10 Minute Farro, cooked according to package directions)

¼ cup chopped fresh parsley

¼ cup chopped fresh chives

4½ ounces goat cheese (about ⅔ cup)

Grated zest of ½ lemon

1 garlic clove, pressed

Kosher salt and freshly ground black pepper to taste

4 red bell peppers (about 8 ounces each), halved lengthwise, seeded, and deribbed

2 bunches scallions, trimmed but left whole

2 tablespoons extra-virgin olive oil, plus more as needed

¼ cup dried bread crumbs

4 large eggs (optional), fried

Hot sauce, for serving

TO VEGANIZE: REPLACE THE GOAT CHEESE WITH 2 TABLESPOONS NUTRITIONAL YEAST AND OMIT THE EGGS

1 Preheat the oven to 400°F.

2 In a large bowl, combine the farro, parsley, chives, goat cheese, lemon zest, garlic, and salt and black pepper. Fill the bell pepper halves with the farro mixture. Arrange the pepper halves in a baking dish just large enough to hold them. Add ½ cup water to the baking dish.

3 In the same bowl that you mixed the filling in, toss the scallions with 1 tablespoon of the olive oil and salt and pepper. Set aside.

4 Cover the pepper-filled baking dish with aluminum foil and bake until the peppers are tender, 35 to 40 minutes.

5 Meanwhile, in a small bowl, toss the bread crumbs with the remaining olive oil and salt and pepper.

6 Remove the foil from the baking dish, sprinkle the tops of the peppers with the bread crumbs, and return to the oven. Bake, uncovered, until the bread crumbs are golden and the peppers are very tender, 10 to 15 minutes.

7 Meanwhile, in a nonstick skillet, heat the scallions over medium-high heat. Cook, tossing, until charred, about 3 minutes. Remove and chop.

8 If you're making this with eggs, reduce the heat under the same skillet to medium-low, adding oil if the pan is dry. Crack each egg into a small bowl and then gently slide the egg into the pan. From this point, you want to cook the eggs for 3 minutes, making little dashes in the whites with your spatula in the first minute or so to help the top part cook. Once the whites are mostly set, cover the pan for 30 seconds. Using a spatula, gently remove the eggs from the pan. This is for sunny-side up eggs. Flip them and/or cook longer if you want over easy fried eggs.

9 Serve 2 pepper halves per person, topping one of them with a fried egg. Garnish with chopped scallions and pass hot sauce at the table.

Hooks

or

More sauces, sides,
and sparkly things
that add
major flavor
to your
Vegetarian cooking

Recipes

IN MY FIRST VOLUME OF *THE WEEKDAY VEGETARIANS,* I talked about the idea of always having a "hook," or one slightly indulgent thing on the plate that you or your diners can get excited about. That might mean something carby, like a crispy, garlicky grilled bread rubbed with fresh tomatoes, or creamy scalloped potatoes. It could also just be the small but spectacular act of topping a green salad with sweet-and-salty almond clusters. Or, it might be as simple as deploying a sauce or a glaze or a dressing or piling dinner on top of a bed of whipped vegetable or cheese, which immediately ups the deliciousness factor as well as the *drama* factor. All of these things address an issue that you may have come up against in your vegetarian cooking, namely: How do you compensate for the missing animal fat, i.e., that most reliable crutch for deep, dimensional, addictive flavor? The answer, at least partly, is in the following pages. You'll notice that the MVPs of umami and creaminess and mouthfeel are all here: soy sauce, spicy chili-tomato pastes and related products (harissa, chile-garlic sauce), lime juice, lemon juice, vinegars, nutritional yeast, miso, tahini, and avocado. Next time you are drawing up that shopping list, make sure they are right on top.

Champagne Vinaigrette

VEGAN

MAKES ⅔ CUP

This one is bright and delicate and very everyday in its simplicity, perfect to use when you don't want to mess too much with the flavor of super-fresh vegetables or greens, and with a simple green salad, especially one made with arugula, pea shoots, chicory, Gem and/or Bibb lettuce, and spinach. If you don't have champagne vinegar, feel free to swap in white wine vinegar.

⅓ cup extra-virgin olive oil

¼ cup champagne vinegar

1 teaspoon Dijon mustard

1 small garlic clove, pressed

Kosher salt and freshly ground black pepper to taste

In a small bowl or screw-top jar, combine the olive oil, vinegar, mustard, garlic, and salt and pepper and whisk or shake until emulsified and smooth. Refrigerate in an airtight container for up to 5 days.

Peanut-Lime Dressing

VEGAN

MAKES
ALMOST
1 CUP

I love the flavor of a peanut dressing, but not always the richness. This version is light and easy to drizzle, and the lime adds a nice brightness. Use drizzled on tofu, in green salads, over steamed vegetables like spinach or asparagus, and for the Sugar Snap Pea Salad (page 74).

⅓ cup peanut butter

⅓ cup unseasoned rice vinegar

2 tablespoons soy sauce

1 tablespoon fresh lime juice

2 tablespoons brown sugar

1 tablespoon sriracha

1 large garlic clove, chopped

In a blender or food processor, combine the peanut butter, vinegar, soy sauce, lime juice, brown sugar, sriracha, and garlic and blend until smooth. If the sauce is too gloppy (and not drizzly), process in a tablespoon of water at a time until you reach the desired consistency. Use immediately or store in the refrigerator in an airtight container for up to 5 days.

Sweet and Spicy Tahini Dressing

MAKES 1 CUP

Tahini is a gift from the gods for vegans (and people feeding vegans) and non-vegans alike. It lends anything a touch of creamy nuttiness. (I love Soom brand for its silky, pourable consistency.) Regarding the harissa, be sure to test it for spiciness before you add it to the dressing—I find all brands have slightly different heat levels. Use this drizzled on the Kale & Roasted Delicata Squash Salad (see page 52), the Crispy Eggplant Bowls with Pistachios & Basil (page 146), roasted cauliflower, roasted cabbage, tossed with steamed spinach, in green salads, or drizzled over tomato salads with sesame seeds.

½ cup tahini

⅓ cup warm water

2 tablespoons fresh lemon juice

2 tablespoons honey or maple syrup

1½ teaspoons harissa paste (test for spiciness, they are all slightly different)

1 small garlic clove, pressed

Kosher salt and freshly ground black pepper to taste

In a blender or mini food processor, combine the tahini, warm water, lemon juice, honey, harissa, garlic, and salt and pepper and whirl until it comes together. If it seizes, keep going; it will eventually smooth out into a dressing-like consistency. Use immediately or refrigerate in an airtight container for up to 1 week.

TO VEGANIZE: REPLACE THE HONEY WITH MAPLE SYRUP.

Yogurt-Dill Dressing

MAKES ²/₃ CUP

This is the dressing you want in your arsenal all year long, but especially in the summer when the Weber is fired up. I love the way the cool yogurt contrasts with the charred smokiness of anything grilled. Use with the Blasted Artichokes (see page 67), green salads, over roasted carrots, roasted or grilled caramelized cabbage, grilled kale, or added to a fresh tomato salad.

½ cup plain whole-milk yogurt or nondairy yogurt

¼ cup chopped fresh dill

2 tablespoons extra-virgin olive oil

2 tablespoons fresh lemon juice

2 medium scallions, white and light-green parts only, roughly chopped

Kosher salt and freshly ground black pepper to taste

In a blender or mini food processor, combine the yogurt, dill, olive oil, lemon juice, 2 tablespoons water, the scallions, and salt and pepper and blend until creamy and smooth, adding more water until the sauce reaches your preferred consistency (I like mine loose and drizzly). Refrigerate in an airtight container for up to 5 days.

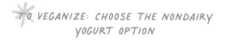

TO VEGANIZE: CHOOSE THE NONDAIRY YOGURT OPTION

Honey-Ta

Yogurt-Shallot Dressing

MAKES
ABOUT ⅔ CUP

This is essentially an all-purpose dressing—but the addition of just a table-spoon of yogurt adds enough tang and creaminess to lend whatever you're eating a slightly luxurious mouthfeel. Use in all salads but especially kale salad.

¼ cup apple cider vinegar

1 tablespoon finely minced shallot

1 tablespoon plain yogurt (preferably whole-milk, but you can use what you have, including nondairy)

1 teaspoon Dijon mustard

1 teaspoon honey or agave

⅓ cup extra-virgin olive oil

In a small measuring cup or screw-top jar, combine the vinegar, shallot, yogurt, mustard, and honey. Whisk or shake to blend. Add the oil and whisk or shake until creamy and smooth. Refrigerate in an airtight container for up to 5 days.

VARIATION: Replace the apple cider vinegar with sherry vinegar and omit the yogurt for a complex, sweet-but-not cloying sherry-shallot vinaigrette (page 209).

TO VEGANIZE: USE THE NONDAIRY YOGURT OPTION AND REPLACE THE HONEY WITH AGAVE

Ginger-Miso Dressing

VEGAN

MAKES ⅔ CUP

I cannot overstate how addictive this dressing is, which is mostly because of the miso. For a long time I was afraid to use too much of it in anything—it's so intensely flavorful—but then I realized it was the ingredient that makes all those otherwise boring salads at the DIY cafes so addictive. So here I use 3 tablespoons instead of my normal 1 or 2. Also the jalapeño lends a deep pepper flavor (in addition to the heat), but you can also use a few drops of chili oil or hot sauce instead. Use in Choose-Your-Own-Adventure Slaw (page 75); toss with tofu, salad greens, and sliced almonds; drizzle on Roasted Vegetables with Miso Butter (page 76, instead of the miso butter); or toss with sugar snap peas, cooked and chilled asparagus, radishes, and chives.

⅓ cup neutral oil, such as grapeseed (olive oil is fine, too, if it's what you've got)

¼ cup seasoned rice vinegar

3 tablespoons sweet white miso

2 teaspoons toasted sesame oil

1 teaspoon brown sugar (light or dark)

2-inch piece fresh ginger, peeled and finely chopped

½ small jalapeño, seeded and chopped

In a mini food processor, combine the neutral oil, rice vinegar, miso, sesame oil, brown sugar, ginger, and jalapeño and whirl until emulsified and smooth. Add water, a tablespoon at a time, if you need to adjust the consistency to be dressing-drizzly. Refrigerate in an airtight container for up to 2 weeks.

Soy-Lime Dressing

VEGAN

MAKES ²/₃ CUP

This is one of those light dressings that sparks the simplest vegetable dish without overpowering it. I love it with steamed spring vegetables, in the Choose-Your-Own-Adventure Slaw (page 75), tossed with sprout salads, Gem lettuce salads, chilled noodle dishes, or drizzled over steamed bok choy, asparagus, sugar snap peas, and avocados.

¼ cup neutral oil, such as grapeseed (olive oil is fine, too, if it's what you've got)

3 tablespoons fresh lime juice

2 tablespoons seasoned rice vinegar

1 tablespoon soy sauce or tamari

½ teaspoon sriracha

Dash of toasted sesame oil

In a small bowl or screw-top jar, combine the neutral oil, lime juice, vinegar, soy sauce, sriracha, and sesame oil and whisk or shake until emulsified and smooth. Refrigerate in an airtight container for up to 5 days.

Honey-Sea Salt Almonds

MAKES 1 CUP

These pack a flavor punch that's way more than the sum of their (very few!) parts. Use in salads with stinky cheese like Gorgonzola, on yogurt, and for a snacky starter/cheese board.

1 cup sliced almonds

Flaky sea salt (about ½ teaspoon)

2 tablespoons extra-virgin olive oil (or enough to coat, not drench)

1 tablespoon honey, plus maybe a little more

1   Preheat the oven to 350°F. Line a sheet pan with parchment paper.

2   Spread the almonds on the lined pan, then sprinkle with sea salt and drizzle with the olive oil and honey, mixing together with your hands so all the nuts are mostly coated. It's okay if some are close together—those will become yummy clusters.

3   Bake until slightly deeper in color, being careful not to burn, 6 to 8 minutes. Let cool. Store in a covered jar or airtight container for up to 2 weeks.

Jam-Jar Pickled Chiles

VEGAN

MAKES 1 CUP

Here, you get to bypass the stovetop—some vigorous shaking of the jar with the pickling liquid is enough to dissolve the sugar. Use on top of Butternut Squash Galette with Feta & Chiles (page 119), Coconut-Corn Soup with Tofu, Basil & Chiles (page 46), Crispy Pan-Fried Gnocchi with Peas & Chiles (page 163), on pizzas, in tacos, added to salads, and even to tarts.

3 tablespoons distilled white vinegar

1 tablespoon sugar

½ cup warm water

1 medium garlic clove, halved

2 to 3 chiles, such as serrano, bird's eye, Fresno, or ají amarillo, thinly sliced, seeded to desired heat preference

In a jam jar or other half-pint screw-top jar, combine the vinegar, sugar, and warm water. Shake vigorously until the sugar dissolves, about 20 seconds. Add the garlic and chiles. They can be ready to use in 30 minutes, but are better the longer they sit. Refrigerate for up to 1 week.

Jammy Tomatoes

VEGAN

**MAKES
1 TO 2 CUPS**

These are critical to the Lentil Salad with Jammy Tomatoes & Feta (page 133) and are also wonderful on top of braised beans, pastas, or as a topping for Whipped Feta (page 231), or just plain chilled full-fat Greek yogurt that's been spread on a plate like icing on a cake. The slow, 90-minute cook time is what gives the tomatoes their sweet, concentrated flavor, but if you don't have time, you'll get something close if you roast them at 300°F for 1 hour.

**2 pounds
Roma tomatoes,**
quartered (or
halved cherry
or grape)

**2 tablespoons
extra-virgin
olive oil**

**Kosher salt and
freshly ground
black pepper**
to taste

6 to 7 thyme sprigs
(optional)

1   Preheat the oven to 275°F. Line a sheet pan with foil or parchment paper.

2   In a bowl, toss the tomatoes with the olive oil and season with salt and pepper. Arrange them skin-side down on the lined sheet pan, tucking thyme sprigs (if using) in between the tomatoes. Bake until they are shriveled and deep red, about 1½ hours.

3   Let cool, then refrigerate in an airtight container for up to 5 days.

Rice Vinegar–Pickled Cabbage

VEGAN

MAKES 1 CUP

I often swap in red wine vinegar or apple cider vinegar, but I find using rice vinegar is the most surprising while still being very versatile. Use on Miso-Mushroom Tacos (page 195), Smoky Black Bean Bowls with Herby Eggs & Avocado (page 154), or on top of any tacos or sandwiches.

⅓ **cup unseasoned rice vinegar**

3 tablespoons sugar

2 teaspoons kosher salt

3 cups shredded cabbage (red is my favorite, but you can use any kind: green, napa, savoy)

¼ **teaspoon red pepper flakes**

1   In a heavy medium saucepan, combine the vinegar, sugar, salt, and 2½ cups water and bring to a boil over high heat, stirring occasionally. When the sugar has dissolved, add the shredded cabbage and pepper flakes, reduce the heat to low, and simmer, uncovered, until the shreds have wilted, about 4 minutes.

2   Remove the pan from the heat and set aside to cool to room temp. You can use the pickled cabbage immediately or chill in an airtight container for up to 7 days.

Grilled Bread

VEGAN

MAKES 4 SLICES

Are you thinking: A recipe for . . . essentially . . . toast? Really? Yes, really. Hardly a night goes by in the summer when we're not transforming a ho-hum, nearly-stale loaf into a plate of smoky, charred slices that are the last thing to go on the grill, but the first to disappear at the table. A few favorite ways to enjoy: Use as a base for creamy cheeses and fresh vegetables for open-face tartines; serve alongside all soups (pages 37 to 50); or with the Whipped Feta (page 231); or rub garlic and tomatoes across it for easy pan con tomate.

1 large garlic clove (optional), halved

4 slices (¾ inch thick) crusty bread, such as peasant or boule (sourdough or white)

¼ cup extra-virgin olive oil

Kosher salt to taste

If using garlic, rub it along the crusts of the bread, then rub each slice of bread with the roughed-up side of the garlic clove. (This helps release the garlic "juice.") Brush one side with olive oil and place that side on the grill. While they toast, brush the top side with more oil. After about 30 seconds, flip the bread and toast on the other side. Transfer from the grill onto a platter and season lightly with salt. Eat right away.

Crispy Capers

VEGAN

MAKES ½ CUP

Honestly, capers that are straight out of the jar usually provide a good briny pop however you are using them. Crisping them up, though, takes them to another level in terms of texture, lending salads, soups, and pastas an airy crispiness. Use in the Shells with Artichoke Sauce & Crispy Capers (page 167), on Sliced Avocado Salad with Arugula & Crispy Capers (page 73), and anything that begs for bite, from rich pastas to creamy soups and salads.

¼ cup extra-virgin olive oil

½ cup brined capers, drained and patted dry

1   In a small to medium skillet, heat the oil over medium heat until it looks shiny, about 1 minute. Add the capers and cook until they get golden and crispy, about 3 minutes, stirring halfway through.

2   Using a slotted spoon, transfer them to a paper towel and drain. Store in an airtight container at room temperature for a day. You can store them for up to 3 days, but they are best eaten at their crispiest, aka, right away.

Frizzled Onions

MAKES ½ CUP Different from caramelized onions, which are sticky and sweet, the point of these crispy fried onions is to add a little texture alongside the almost burnt-caramel flavor—think about them for those nights when you wish you had the can of fried onions. Use in Pureed Broccoli Soup with Romesco & Frizzled Onions (page 44), Smoky Tomato-White Bean Soup (page 38), Brown Butter Orzo with Zucchini & Basil (page 174), soups, tacos, and sandwiches.

2 tablespoons unsalted butter

2 tablespoons extra-virgin olive oil

1 large yellow onion, halved and thinly sliced

Kosher salt and freshly ground black pepper to taste

In a medium skillet, heat the butter and olive oil over medium-high heat. Once the butter is melted, add the onion, season with salt and pepper, and cook, stirring only occasionally, so they get deeply browned but not burned, 8 to 10 minutes. These are best eaten right away to preserve crispiness, but if you have leftover, store in an airtight container for up to 1 week, and recrisp in a hot skillet (no oil necessary) for 2 minutes.

TO VEGANIZE: REPLACE THE BUTTER WITH OLIVE OIL

Spicy Avo Sauce

VEGAN

MAKES 1½ CUPS

This is a vegan take on a Peruvian green sauce I first learned about from cookbook writer and influencer Gina Homolka. Initially, I leaned on it heavily when serving grilled fish and chicken to dinner guests, but eventually realized it had a magical effect—elevating so many of my everyday go-tos, from eggs to grain bowls. This is wonderful as a bed for vegetables (any and all, roasted, grilled, or fresh), or grilled Halloumi or baked feta; or instead of mayo in a veggie sandwich; or, when thinned out with a little water, drizzled on top of Tamarind-Glazed Cauliflower Tacos (page 182).

2 cups loosely packed fresh cilantro, including stems

¼ cup roughy chopped red onion

¼ cup salted roasted pumpkin seeds (pepitas)

3 tablespoons extra-virgin olive oil

2 tablespoons distilled white vinegar

1 heaping tablespoon Dijon or yellow mustard

1 small garlic clove, peeled but whole

1 jalapeño, seeded and chopped

Kosher salt and freshly ground black pepper to taste

2 avocados, halved and pitted

1   In a food processor or blender, combine the cilantro, onion, pumpkin seeds, ¼ cup water, the olive oil, vinegar, mustard, garlic, jalapeño, and salt and pepper to taste and pulse a few times to break down.

2   Scoop the avocado into the mixture, pulsing again until combined, but not completely pureed. You're going for a consistency that's thinner than guacamole but thicker than salad dressing. If it looks too thick, taste, and add water to thin. Taste for seasoning and refrigerate until ready to use. It will keep in an airtight container for up to 5 days.

Romesco Sauce

VEGAN

MAKES 1 CUP

This was buried inside a cauliflower recipe in my first book, but I'm giving it its own recipe here because I found myself turning to it often to punch up so many vegetables and bean bowls and salads. It's also 100-percent vegan. Use dolloped on Pureed Broccoli Soup with Romesco & Frizzled Onions (page 44), as a bed, spread under roasted cauliflower, on top of brothy white beans, tossed with pasta, spread on Grilled Bread (page 221), and atop grilled or fried eggplant and zucchini.

1 (12-ounce) jar roasted sweet red peppers, completely drained

1 garlic clove, peeled but whole

½ cup blanched sliced almonds

⅓ cup extra-virgin olive oil

2 teaspoons red wine vinegar

Kosher salt and freshly ground black pepper to taste

In a blender or small food processor, combine the roasted peppers, garlic, almonds, olive oil, vinegar, and salt and pepper and blend until emulsified. You want the sauce to be spreadable, so it should be on the thicker, chunkier side. Refrigerate in an airtight container for up to 10 days.

Arugula Pesto

VEGAN

MAKES ¾ CUP

This vibrant green sauce serves a few purposes—a nice bright and peppery hit for the taste buds if you're eating something rich, creamy, or cheesy. But it's also incredibly beautiful and when served either dolloped on top of something or spread underneath like a bed it ups the wow factor of just about anything, from Spicy Feta Chickpea Wedges with Arugula Pesto (page 84) to risotto to creamy soups and cheesy toasts. If you want to make a traditional pesto, you can sub in the same amount of basil for the arugula.

2 cups packed arugula

⅓ cup extra-virgin olive oil

3 tablespoons walnuts or pine nuts, toasted

2 tablespoons fresh lemon juice

Kosher salt and freshly ground black pepper to taste

In a mini food processor or blender, combine the arugula, olive oil, nuts, ¼ cup water, the lemon juice, and some salt and pepper and process until smooth and bright green. Refrigerate in an airtight container for up to 3 days.

Herby Artichoke Sauce

VEGAN

MAKES 3 CUPS It never gets old, whirling a humble can of artichokes with a few aromatics to yield a silky, no-cream creamy sauce. Use in the Shells with Artichoke Sauce & Crispy Capers (page 167) or as a bed under roasted Brussels sprouts or pan-seared broccoli.

2 (14-ounce) cans artichoke hearts (quartered, halved, whatever), drained

3 scallions, white and light green parts only, roughly chopped

½ cup extra-virgin olive oil

1 tablespoon fresh lemon juice

Kosher salt and freshly ground black pepper to taste

Handful of chives, basil, tarragon, dill, or mint (solo or as a combo), roughly torn or chopped

In a blender or food processor, combine the artichokes, scallions, olive oil, lemon juice, salt and pepper, and herbs (any combination, but my favorite is straight basil), and give it a whirl until it's emulsified and saucy, 15 to 20 seconds. You will probably have to scrape down the sides halfway through. It should be the consistency of super-smooth, pourable hummus. Pour into a bowl or jar. Store in the refrigerator in an airtight container for up to 1 week.

Whipped Feta

MAKES 1 1/2 CUPS

Of all the beds in this section, I'd call this the most supremely indulgent one. I'm not saying there is anything wrong with that, but if this is on the table, you don't need much more than a simple salad, and some good crusty bread . . . but if you wanted to err on the side of even more satisfying, may I suggest serving it under Jammy Tomatoes (page 218), Pomegranate-Glazed Eggplant (page 71), or grilled zucchini, or with a drizzle of hot honey, black pepper, mint, and some crusty bread or crackers.

8 ounces feta cheese, preferably French (which is typically creamier than Greek)

4 ounces cream cheese (whipped or regular)

2 tablespoons extra-virgin olive oil

Freshly ground black pepper to taste

Up to 2 tablespoons milk, cream, or water

1   In a food processor, combine the feta, cream cheese, olive oil, and pepper and process until smooth and fluffy, about 30 seconds. Add the milk a drizzle at a time (up to 2 tablespoons) if it is too thick. You want the spread to be airy and light.

2   Using a large spoon, scoop the cheese into a shallow bowl and spread it out like frosting, using the back of the spoon to make a slight well in the center that's thicker on the sides than on the bottom. If saving for later, store in an airtight container in the refrigerator for up to 5 days.

ACKNOWLEDGMENTS

Like they say, simplicity is hard work, and it takes a lot of people to make something look easy. That is 1,000 percent the case with the book you are holding in your hands and to that end, I'd like to express my gratitude to the following friends and colleagues:

The Clarkson Potter team: my editor, Raquel Pelzel, for her all-will-be-well energy, and for being excellent at both in-the-weeds editing and big-picture thinking; art director and designer Stephanie Huntwork for her astute eye and for always saying "messier" or "more dynamic" when we are on set; copy editor Kate Slate for wrangling a mess of words and recipes into a clean, consistent manuscript. Editorial assistant Elaine Hennig for all the things she does behind the scenes that I will probably never know about. In publicity and marketing, Lauren Chung and Andrea Portanova for always making sure the message gets out and gets out well. And Francis Lam and Aaron Wehner for their continued support and enthusiasm.

The Photography squad: photographer Christine Han, my rock, my partner, my dear friend whose vision for my projects I trust more than my own; food stylist Lauren Radel, who made all my recipes look like their best selves; Maeve Sheridan, the most generous prop stylist in the business; and digital tech assistant Stephanie Munguia, who helped out on days off from her full-time job. You're a real one, Steph!

My agent, Elyse Cheney, for always having my back; a few generous neighbors: Jess Galen, who came through in the clutch on photo shoot day with olive oil that was the exact color of grassy green I needed; Sonya Terjanian for handing me a huge bag of museum-worthy heirloom tomatoes straight from her garden a half hour after I texted her "Tomato Emergency! Help!" Robin Helman, for her tomato tart triage. Ron Turcios, the Baddest Ever, for his crucial last-minute taste testing. Olivia Mack McCool for so many things, but specifically for teaching this old dog new social media tricks. For the *Cup of Jo* squad: Jannelle Sanchez, Maureen Heffernan, Kaitlyn Teer, and of course, our fearless captain, Joanna Goddard. Everything is more fun when you're all weighing in on things. (And not just on work things!)

For my Substack Community: In December 2020, I was in a parking lot waiting for my daughter to finish "socially-distanced" soccer practice when I received an email from a Substack rep asking me if I was interested in starting a newsletter on their platform. In a very uncharacteristic move, I replied yes immediately, and it somehow turned into one of the smartest professional decisions I ever made. Thank you to Dan Stone, who helped shepherd me through the process of launching and beyond, and to everyone who has subscribed to the *Dinner: A Love Story* Substack newsletter. I love the tight, positive, supportive community we have built together! Special shout-out to reader Ashley Perault, who won the recipe testing contest I held on Substack—it's because of her that I added Gruyère to the frittata on page 91.

To the Fammy Fam: Abby, Phoebe, and Andy, who inspire me to live and love big every day. By now, you know the rule: Joy was not made to be a crumb.

Index